A HISTORY OF
FIRE-FIGHTING
AND EQUIPMENT

Copy Editor : William J. Howell
Art Editor : Deborah Miles
Design : Mark Holt

This edition published in 1978 by
New English Library Limited
Barnard's Inn, Holborn, London EC1N 2JR, England

© Text and illustrations copyright New English Library Limited 1978

Set in Monotype Univers
Text by Hunt Barnard Printing Ltd
Captions by South Bucks Typesetters Limited
Printed by Fratelli Spada, Ciampino, Rome, Italy

450 03947 1

**Endpapers: The New York Fire
Insurance Patrol of 1876; from
'Harper's Weekly', 4 March 1976.**

**Facing page 1: Steam-powered fire
engine in service with the Spokane
Fire Department, Washington, in the
1890s.**

A HISTORY OF
FIRE-FIGHTING

BY ARTHUR INGRAM

AND EQUIPMENT

The author and the publishers wish to acknowledge the assistance rendered by all the manufacturers who have so willingly supplied photographs and other material for this work. The photographic credits detail the individual suppliers, but the author is especially grateful to Bryan Edwards and Robert E. Graham for allowing access to their personal collections. Thanks also go to Lieutenant Arthur J. Carr of the New York Fire Department for his friendly advice and co-operation, and to Carmichael Fire and Bulk Ltd; Oshkosh Truck Corporation, and Simon Engineering Dudley Ltd for the use of material relating to their particular products.

Illustrations have been supplied by:

Alvis Ltd; American History Picture Library; American La France; American Museum of Fire Fighting; Australian Historical Society of Fire Engines; Sven Bengston; Boyer Town; British Leyland; Calavar Corporation; Camiva; Carmichael Fire and Bulk; Chubb Fire Equipment; Maurice Cole; Daimler Benz; Bryan Edwards; Fire-X Corporation; Ford Motor Co; G. H. Georgano; Robert E. Graham; HCB-Angus; F. Hediger; Hestair-Dennis; Hino Motors; Imperial War Museum, London; Arthur Ingram; Klockner-Humbolt-Deutz; London Fire Brigade Museum; Mack Trucks; Magirus-Deutz; Magirus, Ulm; Merryweather & Sons; Carl Metz; MOWAG; New York Fire Department; 'Old Motor' magazine; Adam Opel; Oshkosh Truck Corporation; Pierce Fire Equipment; Presha Fire Equipment; Pyrene; RAF Fire Service; Gordon Rogers; Rosenbauer; Anton Ruthmann; Saval-Kronenburg; Salvani Anticendi; Science Museum, London; SIDES; Simon Engineering; Sisu, Finland; Skuteng; John Thompson; Total; Vauxhall Motors; Ward La France; Waterous Co.

CONTENTS

Early Equipment   7

The Steam Era   13

Self-propelled Fire Engines   22

Motor Vehicles   31

The Streamlined Era   40

The War and After   52

Today and Tomorrow   63

Aircraft Crash Trucks   76

Building a Fire Engine   95

The Fire-fighters   104

Special Risks   118

This picture: Parade of the Fire Department, New York City, in 1866; from 'Harper's Weekly', 8 December 1866.

Six thousand years ago, we are told, there was a fire brigade in China. After that, our knowledge of early man's constant struggle to control fire, which was as great an enemy as friend, is rather sketchy. Control to some degree there certainly was, or the cities of ancient civilisation would frequently have been destroyed.

We must also assume that if in early times a fire was not immediately doused with water thrown from some handy container it was left to burn itself out. Little could be done with the small amounts of water that could be held by cooking vessels or other homely receptacles made of pottery that were in general use before buckets, even if they happened to be filled with water when fire broke out.

The Romans guarded against fire by ordering every householder to keep buckets, syringes, hooks and mops ready. Such household tools were probably the chief means of fighting fires before the introduction of large pumps on fire engines. The long-handled hooks were used to pull burning roofs down to the ground where the fire could more easily be put out. Other early hand-equipment included large and heavy hammers which served to demolish or break open a building, or perhaps even to make a fire-break. Simple ladders gave access to roofs; the humble bucket was essential, and the well-known fireman's axe has remained unchallenged to this day as a tool unrivalled in securing quick entry through locked doors.

However, early equipment was not wholly primitive. Pliny the Elder used the word *sipho* to describe fire engines, but it is not clear whether he meant a large double-cylinder pump or a small hand-held syringe. Certainly at that time there existed a simple siphon-squirt or syringe that sucked up water from a container and squirted it at the fire. Pliny's

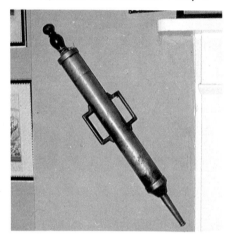

sipho was undoubtedly used during the Roman occupation of Britain and after the Romans left. The squirts used in Britain up to the seventeenth century were little changed from earlier patterns.

Another Roman – the first-century architect and engineer Vetruvius – records that a brass fire engine was built by Ctesibius, a Greek inventor who lived in the second century BC. Ctesibius's machine appears to have been the first to employ an enclosed

Facing page: Fire-fighting tools from 'De re Metolica' of Agricola, in 1556.

Left: Almost unchanged since ancient times; 16th-century brass hand-squirt from an old London church.

Below: Hero's engine.

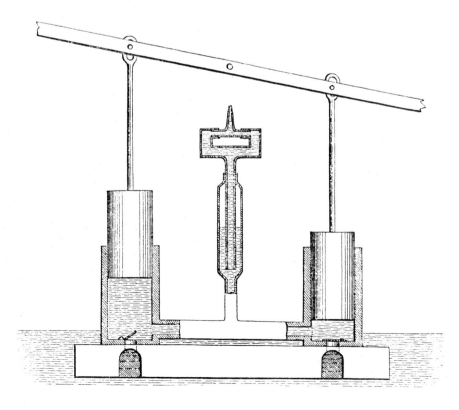

air chamber to produce a continuous flow of water as two pistons worked alternately.

Hero of Alexandria, who was a pupil of Ctesibius, adopted Ctesibius's design when he constructed an engine with two vertical cylinders which worked on their downward strokes and had a small air vessel to provide a continuous flow of water for as long as the pumps were working. The machine had a discharge pipe which was fitted with a swivel joint so that the water could be directed at the fire. This device became known as a gooseneck and was widely used on manual machines. It is still to be found in the modern monitor used on some fire-fighting equipment today.

The use of mechanical means of fighting fires seems to have been discarded after the fall of the Roman Empire, and to have

remained neglected until interest was revived in 1548 by the publication of a German translation of Hero's work. About the same time, a goldsmith named Anton Plater built a fire engine on wheels in the city of Augsburg – but it was probably an outsize syringe. Even so, it would be interesting to see how the apparatus was charged and emptied.

An engine generally referred to as Lucar's could tell us more about Plater's giant syringe because it followed the same principle, although not exactly as the syringe is known today. If the drawing of Lucar's engine is technically correct, the machine was set up quite close to, and pointed directly at, the fire. The angle of the jet was roughly determined by threading a short rod through a pair of holes in

two supporting quadrants, and a short ladder was then placed beside the filling funnel at the forward end of the syringe barrel. With the ram inside the barrel wound back, the barrel was filled by emptying buckets of water into the funnel, and a tap at the bottom of the funnel was closed. The ram was then wound forward forcibly to create pressure that projected a jet of water from the nozzle. Unless there were several such machines at the site, the fire must often have got the better of the fire-fighters because of the long intervals taken to recharge the barrel.

A different style of engine was described by Salomon de Cause writing in 1615 when, he said, there were many such machines in use in Germany. The engine consisted of an open-topped cask kept filled from buckets. A

force-pump was placed in the centre of the cask, its plunger being attached to a long working lever and pivoting on a vertical post. The upward movement of the pump-plunger caused a valve to open at the bottom of the pump-barrel and allowed water to flow in. As the plunger descended the lower valve was shut and another opened to let the water be forced out along the discharge pipe or gooseneck. This type of pump was hauled on two runners like a sled.

Several other pumps were known in the seventeenth century but the one attributed to John Hautsch of Nuremburg was perhaps the most interesting as it used the principle of an air vessel to maintain a reasonably continuous output. In this design the two cylinders – the pump and the air vessel – were placed side by side inside a copper vessel or cistern which had to be kept filled from buckets. The single-pump cylinder had an inlet valve at the bottom which was opened by the upward movement of the pump-plunger and resulted in the pump-barrel being filled with water. On the downward stroke of the plunger the inlet valve was closed by the pressure of the water which also opened another valve connected to the air vessel alongside. As the water filled the air vessel the air was forced to the top and compressed until the pump-plunger started another upward stroke. Then the valve to the air chamber was closed by the pressure of the water in it, and the compressed air served to expel the water up the vertical discharge pipe to the gooseneck. The pump-plunger was worked up and down by a pair of long hand-levers pivoted on the corner posts of the cistern.

This style of engine must have been made in at least two sizes because one reference states that the engine was carried about on long poles as in the manner of a sedan chair, and another writer of 1655 reported seeing a pump of such dimensions that it required two horses to pull it and twenty-eight men to work the levers. It was said to be carried on a sled 10 ft (3 m) long and 4 ft (1.20 m) wide, and to have a case or cistern 8 ft (2.45 m) long, 2 ft (60 cm) wide and 4 ft (1.20 m) deep. In demonstrations, a height of 80 ft (24 m) was reached with a 1 in. (25 mm) jet.

An engine with two working

Facing page: Lucar's engine.

Below: Hautsch's engine.

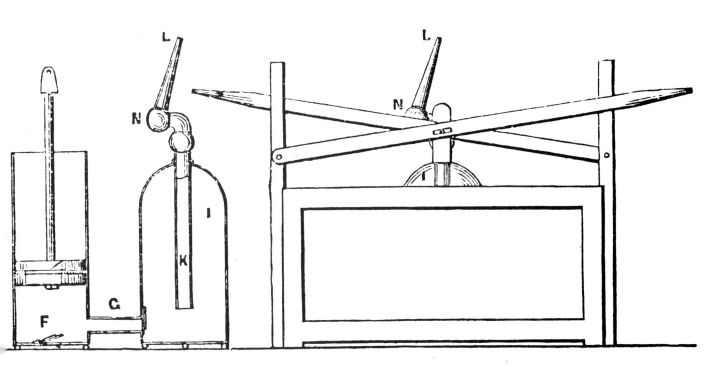

cylinders and an air cylinder was introduced in Paris in 1699 by Dumourier Duperrier, who obtained an exclusive right to manufacture his 'portable pumps' which had cylinders of 4 in. (10.00 cm) diameter and 16 in. (40.00 cm) stroke. As with other contemporary designs, the cylinders were contained within the water-cistern. This type of pump was described by Polinière in 1718 as being so small that difficulty was encountered in keeping it filled by the usual chain of bucket carriers as there was no room to work. Accordingly, the cistern had to be fed from a distance by means of a canvas or sailcloth bag supported in a wooden framework and connected to the cistern by lengths of pipe. Naturally, the remote water supply had to be at a higher level. By 1722 there were thirty such engines in Paris.

An eighteenth-century design of an engine in use at Ypres had a two-cylinder pump without an air vessel but with the long operating handles used in a horizontal or rowing action. This style had storage cisterns on either side of the pumps and was pulled along on a sled-type base.

Another well-known example from the period was the Strasbourg engine which had two cylinders but no air vessel. It was operated by the more usual long levers, and a strictly rhythmical alternation had to be kept if anything like a continuous flow of water was to be discharged.

Richard Newsham of London applied for the first patent for his 'new water engine for the quenching of fires' in 1721. This engine was said to be capable of pumping over 100 gal (455 l) a minute and to possess more cranks and winches than any earlier engine.

Newsham patented another engine in 1725 which, as an improvement on his previous design, had a double-decker style of pump that, in addition to the men on the side levers, required men to stand on the

body of the machine and work treadles with their feet. This engine (like Newsham's earliest design and those of other engineers) included the use of chains and segments to work the pump-pistons – a system that was ridiculed by some of his contemporaries, but it stood the test of time and his engines were undoubtedly successful. A much more important part of his design concerned the manner in which the pump output was increased. In addition to the new leg-power that had been added to arm-power another great attribute was its double-acting pumps – that is to say, an arrangement that pumped water on both up and down strokes. Previous designs

had used only one side of the piston to draw water into the cylinder on the upward stroke, and discharge it by a downward stroke – in other words, a single action.

By 1724 Newsham was announcing himself as an engineer and issuing handbills to extol the virtues and capabilities of his engines. These engines were available in six sizes, and even the largest could be manoeuvred and worked by ten men in a passage about a yard (roughly one metre) wide.

The use of sectors and chains for working the pumps adopted by Newsham had been patented a year earlier by William Mason and Thomas Chamflower, but it is not clear if any engines were built to their system. Newsham's design did not end with double-acting pumps and sectors and chains, and he set about making improvements in details such as placing the working levers to the sides of the

machine so that more men could work them in confined spaces. He also used cranked axles to bring the base of his machine nearer to the ground. He improved the design of a three-way cock whereby the engine could draw water from the cistern or from a remote source – that is, by suction. Another improvement in detail was the use of a fine-thread for the gooseneck pipe joint to make it more watertight and smoother in action.

Most of the designs encountered so far relied upon a supply of water close by – so close in fact that the machines needed to be immersed in the water to work properly. A canvas or sailcloth bucket was the chief means of

transporting water from the supply to the engine and, if the pump was to continue working, the supply had to be almost endless. Ideally, there would be enough people to maintain a line from supply to cistern; a task which was usually done by women while the men were busy at the pumps or tackling the building with hooks and hand-squirts.

Another problem that faced the fire-fighters of the day was to get the pump close enough to the fire to be effective, yet not so close that it was burned, as so many of them were. The early engines were not very big, and most of them were mounted on sleds and not on wheels. When the cistern was full of water the weight of the machine was much greater. The engines that had wheels could not be steered because the body was placed low between the wheels, and the wheels were very close to the body to ease negotiation of the narrow streets, alleys and courtyards of the time.

The greatest step forward in fire-fighting technique, as distinct from the design of engines, came in about 1672 when two Dutchmen, brothers engaged in building fire equipment in Holland, made up some leather hosepipe which was placed between the fire engine and the metal playpipe or nozzle. By this means the fire-fighter was able

to get nearer to the fire without being concerned for the safety of the engine. He was also able to play his jet into the fire with greater accuracy and with swifter movements than when it was fixed to the engine.

The brothers, Nicholas and Jan van der Heijden, had also suggested getting water from a distance by means of the small canvas funnel on a wooden stand to feed the fire engine via a length of pipe. The next step was to get the water out of the canal – common enough in Holland – without having to resort to buckets. To do this they mounted a small suction-pump on the canvas funnel with a length of their pipe going down into the canal. The result was a device with a suction-hose to draw the water up into the funnel, a gravity system to feed the pump, and a pressure-hose to direct the water at the fire. It was a complicated system but it worked, and the van der Heijden brothers were kept busy producing their equipment for Amsterdam, for Holland and for export.

In 1698 the van der Heijdens were successful in arranging a hard section of hose on the *inlet* side of a pump to suck the water inwards direct from the supply. This removed the need for the canvas funnels, wooden stands, small hand suction-pumps, bucket filling and so on. This new suction-hose had to be fairly rigid to prevent it from collapsing as the bucket sucked or exhausted the air from within at the start of operations and so reduced internal pressure before water flowed up the pipe into the pump.

Another necessary requirement of suction-hose was that it should have a larger diameter than the discharge or delivery hose – a larger hose that could pass a great quantity of water at low pressure was found to provide ideal suction. Then the discovery was soon made that the open end of the suction-hose needed to be screened to prevent the ingress of weeds, stones and other matter which could cause damage to the pump and valves. Various types of suction that have included brass, gun-metal, galvanised iron, wire mesh and basket weave have been tried. As pumps have increased their output so the need for a clean water supply has become more important because finer engineering finishes mean closer tolerances which could be ruined by the penetration of stones and debris into the pump and valves. When centrifugal or turbine pumps came into use, clean water became essential, for dirt or gravel drawn from a river acted as an abrasive in the pump and caused untold damage.

Early hoses had sewn seams and screwed metal couplings at the ends of each length for connecting to one another. The use of leather hose spread and gradual improvements took place. The first leather hoses were very heavy, and different kinds of hide were tried to see if a thinner and lighter substance could be obtained. In Britain, a length of hose settled at 40 ft (12.20 m) because it was a convenient size and not unduly heavy. In America, Messrs Sellers and Pennock found that copper rivets were stronger than sewing for the long seam in the hose, and their method was adopted in Europe too.

Leather is certainly a strong material, but it is one that will harden, become inflexible and crack unless it is softened and fed with grease from time to time. To treat leather hoses in that way was unpopular with the men who had to handle them as the grease made the leather slippery and, of course, attractive to dirt.

A 40 ft (12.20 m) coil of leather hose, complete with

Below: 'Old Skiver', an 1812 version of a gooseneck-style side-handled manual pumper. Originally used in New York, it is now on display at the American Museum of Fire Fighting.

Bottom: 'Jefferson No 26', an early 19th-century piano-style manual pumper.

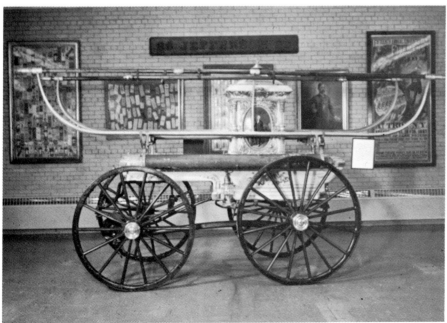

gun-metal couplings at each end and straps for securing it, weighed about 52 lb (24 kg) dry. When charged with water a length of hose contained about 10 gal (45 l) which weighed approximately 100 lb (45 kg). Although a length did not actually have to be carried filled with water, occasions arose when several lengths coupled together and full of water had to be dragged into a building or manhandled while hanging from a ladder.

During the last quarter of the nineteenth century flax hose came into use and was gradually preferred to leather. But prejudices die slowly, and many old fire-fighters looked upon the new material with a jaundiced eye, just as a century later many people viewed plastics with disfavour.

Other equipment and the engines themselves improved gradually in detail during the nineteenth century. Metal valves replaced the old leather type; pump-valves were made more accessible by being placed in a separate chamber; and longer pump-handles, which folded up when the engine was moving, meant that more men could work them. Treadles died out. Engines increased in size, and they had larger wheels and attachments for horse draught. Much of the undergear of the carriage was made from metal instead of wood; springs appeared, and manoeuvrability improved. Sharp corners were removed from runs of pipe; sector and chain mechanism was given up. And engines were made self-sufficient by being fashioned to carry equipment for use at a fire that until then had been kept in buildings. Generally speaking, designs were tidied up and vehicles were made shorter and more manageable.

In 1827 Mr John M. Cooper showed his new rotary engine in the Corporation yard at New York. It was pitted against the engines of the local department and is reported to have pumped more water than the two regular engines put together.

The first steam-powered pump which could be used as a land fire engine was constructed in London in 1829 by John Braithwaite and John Ericsson. Their machine had a vertical boiler at the rear which supplied steam to a ten-horsepower, two-cylinder horizontal engine. The piston rods of this engine were extended to form the rods of the pump at the front of the carriage just behind the driver's seat. The vehicle was equipped for horse traction with large rear wheels and a locking forecarriage. The feedwater was heated by the exhaust steam being piped through it before discharging to the atmosphere. A spherical air chamber was fitted.

From the drawing it is difficult to see whether any fuel was carried on the engine because, in addition to the driver's seat at the front, there appears to be only a seat for the engineman behind the boiler. The machine is shown with one discharge hose attached and a suction connection of similar size on the ground, although the suction connection could doubtlessly have been used to obtain water from a fire-plug.

The machine weighed 2¼ tons (2,286 kg) complete and was capable of pumping 30–40 tons (3,048–4,064 kg) of water an hour, and is said to have thrown a jet

Below: Engraving of an 1860s Lee and Larned style rotary pumper.

of water over 90 ft (27.50 m). Writers of the time say that the engine gave a good account of itself when working voluntarily at fires at the Argyll Rooms, the English Opera House and at Barclay's brewery, but contrary to expectations orders for the engine did not follow. It seemed that no one wanted to pioneer the establishment of a machine which could have ended the employment of large numbers of men in working the manual pumps. Yet, by all accounts, local parishes and insurance companies could have saved themselves vast sums of money that were spent when forty men were employed in shifts to work the engines at large fires. It was estimated that at one fire in London nearly £1,000 was spent on beer to keep the pumpers going for several days!

Another criticism of the steam pump was that it could pump water faster than the supply from fire-plugs and mains. The fact that one steamer could replace two or three manuals seemed to be conveniently forgotten. Other strictures alleged that the machine was too heavy to be moved quickly to a fire, and that the boiler fire would have to be kept going continuously if the engine were to be constantly ready.

Although the fire insurance companies seemed not to be interested in Mr Braithwaite's engine, that was not the case with Barclay's brewery. After the engine had helped to put out the fire it remained in use for pumping liquor and beer for about a month, and put up a good performance while doing so.

Bitterly disappointed that his efforts to produce a worthwhile, powerful fire-pump had been ignored by people who should have known better, Braithwaite stopped sending his pump to fires. After a while he produced a second engine, similar to the first but of only five horsepower and with a single steam cylinder driving a single-cylinder pump.

Still resentful about his treatment in Britain, Braithwaite started his sales campaign by taking his new engine to France. In tests there it was reported to have pumped 27 cu ft (30 cm³) of water per minute with the steam pressure standing at 50 lb/sq in. (22.680 kg/2.5 cm²) and the engine performing forty strokes a minute. The jet was said to have reached a height of 109 ft (33 m) when using a 1 in. (2.5 cm) nozzle. From France the engine was taken to Russia where it put up similar performances.

A third Braithwaite engine went to Liverpool for general pumping duties, but was used for pumping

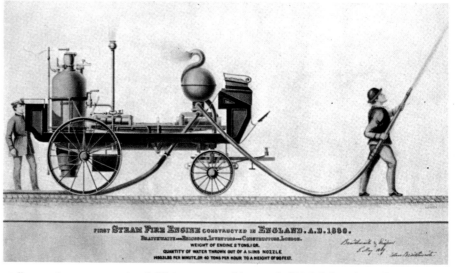

First STEAM FIRE ENGINE constructed in ENGLAND. A.D. 1830.
BRAITHWAITE AND ERICSSON, INVENTORS AND CONSTRUCTORS, LONDON.
WEIGHT OF ENGINE 2 TONS. 1 QR.
QUANTITY OF WATER THROWN OUT OF A 1 INS NOZZLE
1693.3 LBS. PER MINUTE, OR 40 TONS PER HOUR TO A HEIGHT OF 90 FEET.

at fires when so required. This model had a two-cylinder engine that drove a three-cylinder pump by means of gearing and not directly as before. The arrangement of gearing enabled the engine to run at a slower speed than had been the custom.

Braithwaite's journeys in Europe were not in vain, for in 1832 a fourth engine was delivered to the King of Prussia who wanted it to protect the important public buildings of Berlin. This was a larger engine, called *Comet*, of fifteen horsepower with a rear-mounted vertical boiler supplying steam to a horizontal engine. It, too, was of the two-cylinder type but with increased dimensions for the greater power required. The cylinders had a diameter of 12 in. (30 cm) with a 14 in. (35 cm) stroke, and were

coupled to a set of gears driving the two-cylinder pump with cylinders 10½ in. (26.75 cm) diameter and a 14 in. (35 cm) stroke. Connections were provided for four sets of discharge hose and the total weight with a wooden main frame mounted on a set of Jones' patent iron wheels was four tons (4,064 kg).

The *Comet* underwent pre-delivery tests at Paddington Canal in London, and began to pump from a cold start in times varying from thirteen to twenty minutes. Working at a steam pressure of 75 lb/sq in. (34 kg/2.5 cm²) and

Above: Coloured drawing of the world's first steam fire engine built by Braithwaite and Ericsson of London in 1830.

Right: Powerful La France steam pumper – the mainstay of large fire departments between the end of the manual and development of automobile pumpers.

using a 1¼ in. (3.2 cm) nozzle the jet was thrown 115–120 ft (34.50–36 m) vertically with the engine running at eighteen strokes a minute. Several tests were made with varying sizes of jet, various angles of projection and the engine running at different speeds. In general, the engine put up a good performance and was duly sent to Berlin where it was received enthusiastically, and its builder was made an honorary member of the Berlin

Institute into the bargain.

So, London's rejection was acclaimed in Berlin, and Braithwaite must have felt vindicated after his rebuff at home. Another engine was built in 1833, but this was the last. Braithwaitè abandoned fire engines and a void was created that was not to be filled for twenty-five years, when Mr Shand patented his design of steam fire engine – the first of which, ironically, went abroad, this time to Russia.

However, that is to anticipate events, for chronologically the next advance in steamers took place in New York in 1840 when an English engineer, Paul Rapsey Hodge, persuaded several insurance companies that the way to better fire-fighting lay in the use of powerful steam pumps capable of much greater outputs than the contemporary manual engines. Armed with a contract, Hodge set to work on a new engine at his New York works on 12 December 1840 and, with the help of the Matteawan Company to make the wheels and a few other minor parts, completed the engine on 25 April 1841. '

Hodge's engine was not unlike a railroad locomotive in appearance, with a fire-grate at the rear attached to a horizontal boiler and a smoke-stack at the front. The main frames were of wrought iron and ran both sides of the boiler to provide a place for the engineer at the rear and support the two horizontal engine cylinders and two-cylinder double-acting pumps mounted on either side. At the very front of the machine there were two air chambers, one to each cylinder but connected to act as one.

The steam cylinders had a diameter of $9\frac{1}{4}$ in. (23.5 cm) and

14 in. (35 cm) stroke, while the two pump-cylinders had an 8¼ in. (20.6 cm) diameter and a 14 in. (35 cm) stroke. Connections for four hoses were positioned at the front of the pumps and jets of different sizes were provided for use when single, double or quadruple jets were required.

The first trials of the engine took place in the park next to the City Hall in New York with water coming from an underground cistern. In his contract Hodge undertook to produce a single jet 120 ft (36 m) high, and on this occasion, drawing water from a depth of 12 ft (3.65 m), the jet reached a height of 166 ft (50 m). Further trials with sea water were carried out at the Battery, and the engine gave a good account of itself. At about the same time John Ericsson, of the Braithwaite and Ericsson team, came to New York and produced a design for a steam fire engine along the lines of the 1829 machine, but Hodge, when writing to C. F. T. Young in 1865,

said that it was never built.

The drawing of the Hodge engine shows the piston connecting rods bolted to the large-diameter rear wheels. When pumping, the rear of the engine was jacked up and the wheels acted as flywheels, the axle being made in two halves and joined by a sleeve-socket joint. For running on the road the socket joint was released to permit the rear wheels to revolve separately. This could have allowed the steam cylinders to drive the wheels and make the engine partly self-driven, but as this facility was not mentioned by Hodge we must assume that horses were used for traction.

In 1851 W. L. Lay of Philadelphia produced a design for an engine with a rotary pump and, as with Hodge's machine, the rear wheels were to be used as flywheels when the engine was pumping. Lay's interesting innovation was to feed the engine with carbonic acid gas in order to drive it to the fire while the

boiler was getting up steam. Perhaps this answers the point about the Hodge engine being capable of self-propulsion.

A major turning point in fire engine design came in 1853 when A. B. Latta of Cincinnati constructed an engine that was functional and formed the basis for many more in the next few years, although the two main design features were not permanent. Latta's design included a three-wheel layout which provided a good turning circle for the machine, and he made his vehicle self-propelled. The three-wheel layout was not followed for very long and the second feature of being self-propelled was a great step

Below: Fire engine explosion outside the Bowery Theatre, New York City; from 'Frank Leslie's Illustrated Newspaper', 4 July 1868.

Right: Huddersfield Fire Brigade station in the early 1900s and the Merryweather steamer which was named 'Odersfelt', the Roman name the town.

forward at the time, for self-moving vehicles were not produced in any great numbers in America or Europe until almost the end of the nineteenth century. Engineers might not have agreed about three-wheel layout and self-propulsion, but the Latta design was a feasible proposition for a fire engine and was the first really successful design for a steam fire engine.

long! The pump piston rod, as in earlier designs, was a continuation of the engine piston rod and, like the engine, the pump was also of large size: 7 in. (17.5 cm) in diameter and with a 25 in. (62.5 cm) stroke.

Elsewhere in North America Poole and Hunt, of Baltimore, who started their first fire engine in 1858 with a clean-looking design, soon became known as reputable

The best output of the trial was produced by Reaney and Neafie's *Hibernia*, a single-cylinder engine with a 11¼ in. (2.86 cm) diameter and 14 in. (35 cm) stroke, and a pump of 6½ in. (16.25 cm) diameter and 14 in. (35 cm) stroke. From a 1 in. (2.5 cm) nozzle the water reached a height of 181 ft (54 m) and covered a horizontal distance of 254 ft (76 m).

The second-best performance came from *Washington*, by Poole and Hunt, which put up a height of 178 ft (53 m) and distance of 239 ft (78 m). This machine had an engine cylinder measuring 12½ in. (31.25 cm) in the bore with a 12 in. (30 cm) stroke and a pump cylinder of 6 in. (15 cm) diameter and 12 in. (30 cm) stroke. *Washington*'s performance was enhanced by the fact that it weighed less than half of *Hibernia* – 3,582 lb (1,625 kg) against 8,000 lb (3,628 kg).

The next best was *Mechanic*, another Reaney and Neafie engine, which produced jets of 167 ft (50 m) vertical and 203 ft (60 m) horizontal.

In Britain, Shand had built a steam pump in 1858 which had its vertical boiler placed between the rear wheels with the axle encircling the firebox. The engine and pump were mounted vertically behind the driver's seat, which had space beneath it for hose and tools. Another pump was built in 1859 and on test produced a jet 120 ft (36 m) high from a 1 in. (2.5 cm) nozzle.

Merryweather and Sons built their first land steam fire engine, *Deluge*, in 1861. *Deluge*'s boiler was designed by E. Field, who had performed a similar function for a floating fire engine by Merryweather's and was to have a long connection with the firm. *Deluge* had a horizontal cylinder of 9 in. (22.5 cm) bore by 15 in. (38 cm) stroke which was directly connected to the pump cylinder by means of a common rod. The pump cylinder had a 6½ in. (16.25 cm) bore and 15 in. (38 cm) stroke. It was claimed that this engine threw a jet 170 ft

The three-wheel layout was probably discarded in favour of a four-wheel carriage because of instability, and Latta himself produced some four-wheel designs in which the two front wheels were quite close together. The function of self-propulsion (or semi-self-propulsion in some cases because horses were attached for steering) was probably not popular because of the extra mechanical complications required, and because of the need to keep the water 'on the boil', so to speak, in order to achieve a quick turnout. It was far easier to leave the fire laid in the firebox and drop a match down the chimney as the alarm sounded so that steam could be raised as the engine raced to the fire.

Cincinnati was also the home of Abel Shawk who, in 1855, built his first steam pump. A remarkable feature of this engine was that it possessed only one cylinder, which was 11 in. (28 cm) in diameter and 25 in. (62.5 cm)

builders. Before long they were constructing engines in three sizes: No 1, 6,500 lb (2,948 kg); No 2, 560 lb (254 kg) and No 3, 4,500 lb (2,041 kg). In this engine the pump was two-cylinder with one above the other and with their rods attached to a common cross-head driven by the single-cylinder engine. A small flywheel was also provided.

With other engines appearing during the 1850s, the industry reached such proportions that it was possible for a series of trials to be held in Philadelphia during the course of the Agricultural Society Fair at the end of 1859. Eight steam engines from Poole and Hunt, Reaney and Neafie, Merrick & Sons, Hunsworth Eakins & Co, and Lee and Larned took part in trials lasting three days. All had piston-type pumps with the exception of the engine *Southwark* of Lee and Larned, which was a rotary. The engines, put through their paces by their builders, were tried by a panel of three judges.

(51 m) high from a 1¼ in. (32 mm) nozzle. So, after first appearing some thirty years earlier and suffering a long spell of oblivion, the British steam fire engine was about to find a new lease of life. In that it followed a course similar to the American steamer which was largely ignored until it was resuscitated by A. B. Latta after more than a decade of indifferent existence.

The International Exhibition of 1862 held in Hyde Park, London, included the first public competitive trial of steam fire engines to be held in England — although as only two makers, Shand Mason and Merryweather, competed for a medal it was not a particularly exciting event. Merryweather's engine was *Deluge*, which was on show at the exhibition, but Shand Mason were represented by two machines in service with the London Fire Engine Establishment. There was also an American engine at the exhibition from Lee and Larned, but it did not compete.

In the following year another trial was held at the Crystal Palace, at Sydenham in south London, which attracted ten engines; seven British and three American. This competition was arranged by the committee of the London Fire Engine Establishment who separated the entries into two classes — those weighing up to 1½ tons (1,524 kg) and those weighing from 1½ tons to 3 tons (3,048 kg).

In the smaller class the entries were *Torrent* by Merryweather (Great Britain), an un-named engine by Shand Mason (Great Britain) and *Alexandra* by Amoskeag (USA). The entrants in the class for larger engines were *Sutherland* by Merryweather, an un-named engine by Shand Mason, *Sabrina* by Lee and Larned (USA), *Victoria* by Amoskeag, *Manhatten* by Lee and Larned, *Princess of Wales* by William Roberts (Great Britain), and an un-named engine by Gray and Son (Great Britain).

On the night before the trial

Manhattan was being manhandled into position when the handlers lost control on a slope and the engine tore down the incline, crashed into a tree and severely injured the fireman holding the pole. Not to be beaten, the makers' representatives and some workmen set about repairing the engine for the following day's trials. They did well enough for the engine to be present on the trial ground and pump some water for a while, but it had to be withdrawn for fear of causing further damage. The remarkable thing was that it appeared at all, because even after the repairs it still had one flywheel broken and the other cracked, the boiler sheathing badly

crushed, brasswork battered and the forecarriage completely smashed to pieces.

According to C. F. T. Young, who witnessed the event, the 'trials' (they are his quotation marks) were conducted with a high degree of bias and partiality. In their course one member of the committee openly helped a competitor, and a separate test arranged for one competitor in an evening resulted in that competitor being awarded the first prize !

Although the Crystal Palace trials came in for criticism, there seems to have been wholehearted praise for Merryweather's *Sutherland* and the Shand Mason engine in the large class. The Lee

and Larned *Sabrina* had to be withdrawn because of mechanical disarrangement, and *Victoria* by Amoskeag had some technical problems and could not run at full power. Roberts' engine *Princess of Wales* also suffered some mechanical fault and could not perform fully, while the engine entered by Gray and Son was not really finished by the time the trials started and because of trouble with the boiler-tubes could not compete in any of the tests.

In the light class the Merryweather engine *Torrent* – a working engine not specially prepared for the trials – performed as well as it had previously in use at fires in London. Amoskeag's

more worthwhile if all the engines had been woking properly to give a reliable indication of their capabilities. As it was, builders presumably carefully examined their competitors' product to see what they could learn; but in the event little trans-Atlantic trade in steam fire engines developed. The British market liked, and bought, the home-built machines; the American fire departments did the same, and some exports were made by both camps.

A year later, in 1864, trials were again held in Europe. This time the venue was Holland, where so much pioneer work on delivery - hose, suction-hose and efficient fire brigades had taken place

to other towns and trials were repeated, but no prizes were awarded.

In June 1865 a competition for steam fire engines was arranged at Cologne in connection with the International Exhibition held there. This competition achieved a greater international air with two engines from Britain and one each from Germany and the United States.

The Shand Mason (Great Britain) engine was a large-size single-cylinder vertical engine of 10¼ in. (25.625 cm) diameter and 10 in. (25.5 cm) stroke with pump cylinder bore 9¼ in. (23.5 cm) and stroke 10 in. (25.5 cm) and weighed 6,311 lb (2,863 kg). The Merryweather (Great Britain) engine had a single cylinder of 8 in. (20 cm) bore and 18 in. (45 cm) stroke with a 5 in. (12.5 cm) bore by 18 in. (45 cm) stroke pump cylinder. It weighed 3,927 lb (1,781 kg). The German engine, by Moltrecht & Co of Hamburg, had a single horizontal steam cylinder of 6 in. (15 cm) bore and 15 in. (38 cm) stroke driving a pair of double-acting pump cylinders placed on either side of the steam cylinder, and a weight of 3,591 lb (1,629 kg).

The American engine *Victoria*, by the Amoskeag Company, had a single-cylinder vertical engine with a 10½ in. (26.75 cm) bore and 12 in. (30 cm) stroke driving a vertical double-acting pump cylinder 6 in. (15 cm) in bore and with a stroke of 12 in. (30 cm). Its weight was 5,977 lb (2,711 kg).

Meanwhile, in the United States in the 1850s several steam engine builders produced their first designs – Abel Shawk of Cincinnati; Joseph Lowry of Pittsburgh; Lawson and Pearce of Louisville; Silsby Manufacturing Company, Seneca Falls; Poole and Hunt, Baltimore; Ettenger and Edmund, Richmond; Phoenix Ironworks, Charleston; Lee and Larned, New York City; Neafie and Levy, Philadelphia or New York City; and Bean and Scott of Lawrence. Trials of engines continued: sometimes between

Left: Business end of a Shand, Mason steam pump working at a rally in 1969.

Above: Waterous steam pumper No 3 size, late 19th century.

engine *Alexandra* also put up a good performance although it was plagued with numerous splits in the suction-hose. Shand Mason's engine was reported to have been a violent and shaky starter with much priming of the boiler and an inability to lift water in the test, although it was successful in the evening test already described and awarded first prize in its class amid much protest from the other competitors.

The trials would have been much

some two centuries earlier. Unfortunately, the only two entrants for the trials on this occasion were a pair of British machines – a Shand Mason single-cylinder vertical engine and a Merryweather double-cylinder horizontal engine. After three days of show and trial the judges awarded a gold medal to Shand Mason and a silver medal to Merryweather. Not surprisingly, Merryweather's immediately applied for a retrial, alleging that the poor performance of their engine was due to salt deposits in the boiler and engine, but the judges refused to allow fresh trials. The two engines were then taken

only two competitors trying to win a contract for a particular city company, or larger affairs held at county and State fairs in different parts. In 1860 a single-cylinder, double-pump engine by Ettenger and Edmond of Richmond was tested and threw a $1\frac{1}{2}$ in. (3.75 cm) jet to a distance of 250 ft (76 m). A Lee and Larned engine produced a jet which covered 260 ft (80 m) and a smaller Neafie and Levy engine managed 248 ft (76 m).

Most of the engines at this time were piston pumpers employing either a single- or double-cylinder engine driving a single double-acting pump — although there were some that used a double-cylinder engine and others had a piston engine to drive a rotary pump. Engines were sorted into classes according to their cylinder and pump size, output, weight and whether they were drawn manually or by horses. A first-class engine could be either a single- or double-cylinder engine with a two-cylinder double-acting pump capable of producing four $\frac{7}{8}$ in. (22 mm) jets, two 1 in. (2.5 cm) or one $1\frac{1}{4}$ in. (3.2 cm) streams over distances of 160 ft (49 m), 200 ft (61 m) and 275 ft (84 m)

respectively. Second-class engines were usually single-cylinder types with outputs proportionately less then those of the first-class size. Later a 'new style' of engine was produced and divided into three classes all being single-cylinder and single-pump type and somewhat lighter in construction than the earlier models.

In the early days of steam-powered pumps it was usual to describe the output of the engines as so many jets of a measured size pumped into a defined vertical or horizontal distance. In trials almost everything measurable

was recorded but it was realised that the flow of water and the distance a jet was thrown were dependent upon many factors which included water supply, the size of suction, size of engine and pump cylinders, speed of engine, steam and water pressure, and even the weather. Gradually the term 'gallons (or litres) per minute' came to be accepted as a general guide to the size or output of a particular pump, and in the new ratings the three sizes of pump were about 600 gal/min (2,727 l/min), 400 gal/min (1,818 l/min) and 300 gal/min (1,364 l/min).

During the 1860s further names were added to the list of engine builders: M. R. Clapp of Seneca Falls (soon to become Clapp and Jones of Hudson); the Manchester Locomotive Works, known earlier as the Amoskeag Manufacturing Co of Manchester (New Hampshire patentees of the Amoskeag boiler as used by Bean and Scott and Hinckley and Drury); E. V. Merrick of Philadelphia; Button Fire Engine Works, and Button and Blake of Waterford, New York; Sheppard Iron Works of Buffalo; Banks of New York City; Taylor of New York City; Ives of Baltimore; Allerton; Juckett and Freeman; Cory; Nussey; Gould, and many more.

Naturally, not all succeeded. As the years went by there were more newcomers, amalgamations, successes and failures, but some, such as Gould, Clapp and Jones, Amoskeag, Button, and Ahrens, were part of the fire engine scene for many years.

Below: There's nothing like a fire engine to enthral children – especially if it's a steam one!

SELF-PROPELLED FIRE ENGINES

The surprising thing about steam fire engines is that so few of them were self-propelled, although they formed the backbone of most larger fire brigades for some fifty years at a time when railway steam locomotives reached an advanced stage of development. One reason for the apparent indifference to progress was probably the fact that in many places the fire engine was operated alongside other non-powered equipment which was drawn by horses. Another likely factor was that the steam pumper was not maintained ready to pump at a minute's notice – it had to be given time to get up steam. In some busy stations a small fire was kept going so that the water in the boiler was not stone cold when the pump was called out, and it was the good engineer who had sufficient head of steam

upon arrival at the fire to start pumping without delay. For self-moving engines a working pressure of steam would have been necessary night and day. Some of the early steamers were, in fact, capable of self-propulsion, but steering and braking caused problems and usually horses were relied upon.

The first steam fire pump was British and was designed by John Braithwaite in 1829. The first self-propelled engine in Europe was also made in London by William Roberts in 1862. Several American makers produced self-propellers before the Roberts machine was built but they are more accurately described as semi-self-propelled because they employed horse traction and steering. However, the Roberts machine is important in fire engine history and, indeed, as an early

road locomotive because it was constructed for use in driving machinery or hoisting loads and haulage if so required.

Like many other steam engines of the mid-nineteenth century the Roberts was three wheeled, no doubt to make turning in confined spaces easier. The machine measured 12 ft 6 in. (3.8 m) in length and 6 ft 4 in. (1.9 m) high, and weighed about 7½ tons (7,620 kg) complete with fuel, water and equipment. The front wheel was 3 ft (91.5 cm) in diameter and the rear wheels 5 ft (1.525 m). A square Benson water-tube boiler was located between the rear wheels and supplied steam to a double vertical engine of 6 in. (15 cm)

Below: A John Player cigarette card of the 1903 Merryweather chemical engine with the petrol engine under the driver's feet.

PLAYER'S CIGARETTES.

"FIRST-AID" APPLIANCE, 1903.

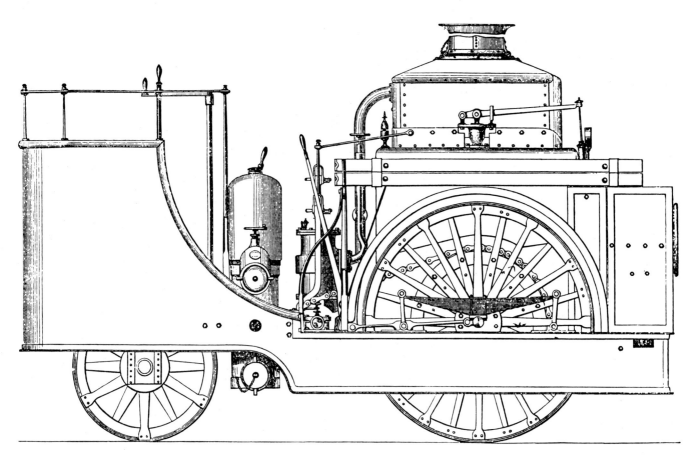

bore and 12 in. (30.5 cm)
stroke which drove the pair of
double-acting pumps of 9 in.
(22.5 cm) bore and 8 in. (20 cm)
stroke. The engine shaft was
fitted with a pulley for driving
machinery and a winch for
hoisting purposes. Drive to the
rear wheels was by pitch chains
that could be easily disengaged on
either side to assist with steering
the machine, which was capable
of being turned in its own length.

One report of the engine in
action recorded that water was
thrown over 140 ft .(43 m) high
and 182 ft (55 m) in distance
through a 1 in. (2.5 cm) nozzle.
Normal road speed was about
12 mph (19 kph) with a maximum
of 18 mph (29 kph) on a level
road. This important machine
was the only self-propeller made by
William Roberts, who found
customers were more willing to

buy types that required separate
traction.

In 1853 A. B. Latta of Cincinnati
built a large three-wheeled
self-propelled steam fire engine
that weighed about 10 tons
(10,160 kg). Although problems
of traction with so heavy a
machine resulted in horses being
used, a company – A. B. & E.
Latta – was formed and several
more machines were built. Most
of the Latta engines were three-
wheeled because of the need for
a machine that was highly
manoeuvrable – although with
their total height approaching 13 ft
(4 m) they had to be turned with
care on uneven surfaces. The
first four-wheeled engine built in
1861 had the low frame swept up
just behind the front wheels to
allow the forecarriage to lock
under; thus earning itself the
reputation of being the first

crane-neck fire apparatus in
America.

When the first Latta machine
was tested in Philadelphia it was
reported to have thrown water for
a distance of 240 ft (73.20 m)
through a 1¾ in. (45 mm) nozzle.
In appearance it looked strangely
like a steamboat, with its tall
chimney high above an unusual
vertical square boiler and a low
frame that swept round the single
front wheel almost hiding it from
view. The positioning of two 6½ in.
(16.5 cm) diameter 24 ft (7.3 m)
long suction-hoses curving round
and almost embracing the
machine added to its maritime
appearance.

The Latta design had the two
rear wheels almost at the extreme
end of the frame just behind the

firebox and vertical water-tube boiler. The two-cylinder engine was located in front of the boiler and the piston rods were extended forward to form the pump-plungers of the two cylinders of the pump. A second machine built in 1854 had the engine mounted across the frame.

Lane and Bodley of Cincinnati adopted the Latta design and built several semi-self-propellers which, like others of the kind, had a degree of self-propulsion at the rear wheels but employed horses for steering and probably to some extent for propulsion.

Another comparatively early manufacturer of self-propellers were the famous Amoskeag company which produced its first in 1867 and last in 1908. Yet, in the forty-one years of continued output only twenty-two machines were produced. As each of the vast engines cost, even in those days, more than $12,000 the demand could not have been great for equipment that only the largest of brigades could afford.

Towards the close of the nineteenth century the steam pump market was dominated by some well-known firms that included the American La France organisation which included Button Fire Engine Works, Silsby Mfg Co, Ahrens Mfg Co, and Clapp and Jones. The American Fire Engine Co was the name adopted for the new group founded in 1891. There were other builders still in the market such as Campbell and Rickards,

Top, left: Turn-of-the-century battery-electric fire pump from Germany.

Centre, left: Rare photograph of an attempted conversion of a horse-drawn steamer by Henry Simonis for the Metropolitan Fire Brigade, London.

Left: Merryweather motor pump for the London Fire Brigade with the 'Hatfield' three-throw piston pump and Aster engine.

Right: A horse-drawn steam pump at Melbourne, Australia, converted by putting an adapted Itala car under the forecarriage.

Jacob Haupt, Hunnemann, Mansfield, Nott, Waterous and Amoskeag. Some of these companies built just a handful of engines while others turned out hundreds during their time. In Britain the steamer market was largely in the hands of such famous concerns as Merryweather and Shand Mason & Co. In Germany the dominant people were Braun, Busch, Krauss, Magirus, Metz and Moltrecht; and elsewhere Knaust was building engines in Austria, Ludwigsberg in Sweden and Thirion in France.

The first self-propelled fire engine in continental Europe would appear to be the Braun of 1890 which was built on the general lines of the British Merryweather and Shand Mason – really a horse-drawn steamer with chain drive to the larger rear wheels, a vertical steering column and a sheet-steel front apron. After Braun there came W. C. F. Busch of Bautzen, who specialised in all forms of pumps, both stationary and mobile, powered by steam, petrol or

electricity. In 1901 Busch produced a steam self-propeller which was similar to Braun's but had twin tie-rods connecting the front axle to the ashpan of the boiler.

Magirus, in 1902, followed the general style of the other self-propelled steam pumps with a vertical boiler just behind the rear axle, a vertical engine immediately behind the driver, and the pump situated below the engine under the chassis frame. Drive was by means of roller chains from a countershaft alongside the engine. During the next few years other steam-powered appliances were produced by Magirus including aerial ladders of 72 ft (22 m).

In the first decade of this century three main sources of power competed with each other for supremacy: steam, electricity from batteries, and petrol, with the petrol-electric hybrid trailing badly in fourth place. More support was given to battery electricity than to its rivals because of its ability to start easily, maintain a constant speed

and take up moderate space on the top of the vehicle. It seems, too, that its popularity, and the unreliability of the early petrol engine, overcame the considerable cost of installation and the inconvenient size and weight of the batteries to the extent that for a few years it had a clear-cut lead over its competitors.

Braun were great advocates of battery electricity and their early publicity material gave details of personnel carriers or *Mannschaftswagen* capable of carrying 1 + 10, electric/steam pumps carrying 1 + 4 and an interesting aerial ladder of 85 ft (26 m) built on the Schappler system of telescoping steel tubes for ladder extension, for which power was supplied by large replaceable cylinders of carbon dioxide.

The Braun range in those early years was based on a battery-electric chassis and included pumps powered by both petrol and steam, personnel carriers and a non-powered 80 ft (24 m) aerial ladder. The traction batteries were located under a

bonnet at the front end and supplied power to a pair of thirteen-horse-power electric motors which drove the front wheels by internal tooth-ring gear.

The Daimler Company also produced a range of fire appliances on both battery-electric and petrol-electric powered chassis. The Lohner-Porsche system was adopted wherein the propulsion motors were built into the front wheels. Personnel carriers, pumps and aerial ladders employing the Schlapper system of telescoping tubes were produced, the latter being powered either by carbon dioxide or compressed air. Other early proponents of the battery-electric system for fire apparatus were Flader, with equipment by Namag; Protos, using the Siemens-Schubert system; Scheele and Busch.

It was almost an invariable custom for electric motors used for propulsion to be mounted at the front wheels, which seemed to be just right for fire engines. However, when Hamburger Feuerwehr modernised their old horse-drawn steam pumps they obtained a battery-electric tractor of the Daimler-Elecktro pattern. This particular vehicle had rear-wheel drive and towed the old steam pump by means of the pump forecarriage being placed on a small low platform at the rear of the tractor. One wonders how this novel approach to the problem worked out in practice.

The very first petrol-propelled vehicle for fire brigade use is generally reckoned to be the 1901 Adler which carried a small pump and hose-reel, some short scaling ladders, and fire hooks, and seated four back to back. Within a few years Opel, Stoewer, Magirus, Daimler, Bussing, Hansa-Lloyd, Durkopp and others produced fire-fighting vehicles and the German motorised fire-fighting industry became one of the most influential and forward thinking in the world.

Towards the close of the last

century two British fire engine builders turned their attention to self-propelled steam pumps – Shand Mason & Co and Merryweather. Their steamers had the usual vertical boilers mounted near the rear of the vehicle with space for the engineer behind. The driver sat right at the front of the vehicle behind a sheet-metal front apron and just behind him there was a box for hose and small tools. The engine and pumps were positioned between the hose-box and the boiler. Although a few of these self-propelled steamers were built, they were not very successful. They were taken into use in London, Bristol, Liverpool, Cardiff, Edinburgh and

nine other brigades in England, and were exported to a dozen countries, but the motor fire engine was soon to make them obsolete. Merryweather's had a larger stake in the market than their rivals and offered six different models, ranging from 300 gal/min (1,363 l/min) up to 1,000 gal/min (4,546 l/min). In London, complaints were made by the public about the vibration caused when the self-propelled engines went past, but this was just after the turn of the century when people were not used to anything much heavier than the local removal van.

Merryweather's also offered a steam-propelled chemical engine

The early fire engines of the petrol-motor era were of the chemical type, there being insufficient power, or reliability, in the early petrol engines to power the pump.

A chemical engine usually consisted of a large copper cylinder of about 50-60 gal (227-272 l) of water which was discharged by gas pressure. The gas was generated by adding bicarbonate of soda to a small amont of sulphuric acid and the ensuing carbonic acid gas was piped to the water-tank where it forced the water along a small-bore rubber hose stored on a hose-reel. A short, scaling ladder was sometimes carried, although the chemical engine was usually accompanied by an escape carrier for the purposes of rescue.

Even before the chemical engines the new motors were tested in the fire service and, as early as 1901, a Daimler tender, with a wagonette-style body presumably just for carrying firemen, was tried out in Liverpool. It was not adopted for use as a fire engine. In the same year the Borough of Eccles experimented with a locally built Bijou light car adapted as a tender capable of carrying a few firemen and short ladder plus tools. Again, this was not a success; probably due to the fact that the chassis was too light and the engine was only seven horsepower.

The established fire engine makers led with reliable equipment. In 1903 Merryweather produced their first motor chemical engine in close collaboration with the Tottenham District Coucil in London. The machine was of twenty horsepower and carried an escape. Next came the first Merryweather motor pump, a thirty-horsepower appliance for Finchley, another London suburb. This machine had a pump with an output of 250 gal/min (1,136 l/min) and carried a detachable wheeled escape. This historic vehicle is preserved in the London Science Museum, although slightly incomplete, through the diligence

and detachable wheeled escape but it is doubtful if any were actually built. This design had the vertical boiler and engine mounted to the rear of the driver to make room for the escape, and the chimney was formed into a large U so that the long escape could nestle inside. Another Merryweather innovation of the period was a battery-electric chemical engine which had the water cylinder under the driver's seat and a hose-bed and standing platform at the rear. A contemporary catalogue advised that these appliances were available because so many towns had electric lighting stations where accumulators could be

Above: Bikkers and Zoom 1905 self-propelled steam fire engine preserved in Holland.

charged. It also mentioned that for operation in hot and damp climates iron wheels should be ordered, evidently because the wooden ones get eaten by ants!

Steam continued to be used in the most powerful fire-pumps right up to the age of the internal combustion engine and, indeed, well into it, for many were attached to, or superimposed on, automobile chassis. Some fire departments were convinced that steam was the best medium for powering fire-pumps, and the last steamers were delivered during the First World War.

of fire service historian T. D. Barclay, who traced it from Finchley to a gravel pit and then to a scrapyard. He told the Science Museum, who negotiated its safe keeping.

Before the advent of the production self-propelled steam and petrol-driven fire engines there were numerous experiments with adapations of old horse-drawn equipment. In 1902 London's Metropolitan Fire Brigade modified one of their horse-drawn steam pumps for self-propulsion, an experiment which showed promise for it worked quite well on good level roads, but was found to be rather underpowered for hilly districts. But after some years the idea was abandoned and the machine returned to its original horse traction.

Another experiment was with articulation, which was attempted by removing the horse-draught pole and forecarriage from a steam pump and putting a Wolseley motor chassis, with fabricated turntable, under the front end of the steamer. This was not a successful operation, for the wheelbase of the tractor unit was much longer than that of the trailer, and, because the old steamer had iron tyres, when the outfit went downhill the tail swung and caused the trailer to come round the tractor. An articulated escape carrier was also planned by Captain Wells of the London brigade, but it is doubtful if it ever went into service. This time, the idea was to build or use an existing four-wheel tractor unit of forward control layout which had its back axle at the extreme rear of the unit. The front pair of wheels were removed from a horsed escape van, and the van was superimposed on the rear of the tractor. From the drawing it looks a clumsy affair and suffers from the same weight and wheelbase problems as the articulated steamer.

Even as late as 1907, when the Merryweather Fire King self-propeller was being built, the London brigade was still trying to

find a suitable means of converting the old horse-drawn equipment to motor traction. Henry Simonis of Walthamstow, who was producing fire equipment at his Pretoria Works and acting as agent for a number of German manufacturers, offered to convert one of the brigade's horsed steamers to self-propulsion. His design was surprisingly different from what might have been expected, for, instead of using the existing steam engine to drive the rear wheels of the machine, he removed the forecarriage completely and in its place put a single front wheel which served to steer and power the appliance. From an old photograph it appears, but is not certain, that the machine was propelled by friction. Driving it must have been a formidable task, considering that the front wheel was carried on a small frame together with the pair of steam cylinders, valve-gear, steam piping, coil-spring suspension – and there were no brakes! Movement forward could be retarded by reversing the engine, and the large rear wheels also had the old type of wood-block-on-rubber-tread handbrake, but after misbehaving itself during demonstrations and overturning, it was converted back to horse traction. This failure did not discourage the resourceful Henry Simonis, for not long after he successfully produced some electrically propelled turntable-ladders for the brigade.

The International Fire Engine Co built some steam-powered hose-wagons at the beginning of the century, but the first gasoline motor pump was the dual-engined Waterous constructed in 1906 for the Radnor Fire Company at Wayne, Pennsylvania. This machine had separate engines for propelling the apparatus and for powering the 300 gal /min (1,363 l/min) pump. It was strictly a pumper, for it carried neither hose nor ladders. Another early builder was the Knox Automobile Co of Springfield, Massachusetts, who produced a soda-acid type

of chemical engine based on a forty-horsepower air-cooled engine chassis. This was soon followed by a whole line of Knox fire equipment. The Webb Motor Fire Apparatus Co started their line of fire apparatus in 1907 and were joined by the Howe Fire

Apparatus Co. Seagrave also began to build motorised fire engines, their first being of the chemical type, and they were soon joined by American La France who produced one the same year but did not immediately undertake series production.

During the next few years the self-propelled motor fire engine was quickly established as the vehicle for fire-fighting, and more builders produced vehicles for fear that they should be left behind by their competitors. Fortunately for them, fire

departments came to see that the petrol engine did not require the attention demanded by horses, or the permanently lit gas jet or small

Below: Waterous motorised fire engine of 1906 with a pump capable of 300 gallons per minute output.

Above: American La France 4-wheel-steering aerial ladder of the motorised ex-horse-drawn type.

fire that was indispensable to busy steamers.

The Robinson Fire Apparatus Mfg Co, and the Anderson Coupling and Fire Supply Co started with a line of motor apparatus. A Locomobile forty-horsepower engine appeared in 1908 and the name Westinghouse was carried on another new engine. Seagrave built their first aerial ladder on a motor chassis in 1909, and in the same year the New York fire department purchased a forty-horsepower Knox high-pressure hose-wagon with a fixed turret, or monitor. This vehicle so impressed the department that within two years plans and requests for finance were advanced to buy 100 pieces of apparatus.

Like many other fire departments, New York had tried converting old equipment to motor power, and although it was reasonably successful for a time, some problems were caused by equipment that was not designed as a whole. Nevertheless, there was great business to be done for a few years during the interim period when many departments wanted up-to-date equipment but had to operate within tight budgets.

Anxious not to let the opportunities of the motor age slip, some of the established

builders offered to supply either two- or four-wheel tractors for attachment to horse apparatus. American La France had their Type 31 two-wheel gasoline tractor which could be bolted direct to the frame of the steamer, aerial ladder or water-tower to make a rigid four-wheel vehicle. Seagrave produced a similar machine. Both these companies also built the more conventional four-wheel tractor units for putting under the front end of old horse equipment, but some enterprising fire departments built their own.

Some most interesting conversion units were offered by companies normally outside the fire equipment business. The Couple Gear Freight Wheel Co of Grand Rapids, Michigan, produced a four-wheel-drive, four-wheel-steering truck based on the gasoline electric system where a four-cylinder engine powered an electric generator which in turn supplied power to four electric motors — one at each wheel. A shortened version of their truck with sloping rear chassis members was supplied to fire departments for attaching to aerial ladders and the like. As each wheel was powered the Couple Gear machine had dual tyres on each wheel.

The Front Drive Motor Co of Hoboken, New Jersey, built many two-wheel tractors for attaching to steam pumps or ladder trucks and they were popular in 1912-

18. They had a short, straight frame with the single axle suspended on half-elliptic springs. Power came from a four-cylinder engine mounted transversely under a small bonnet or hood. This tractor was sold under the name Christie Front-Drive Auto Tractor.

Another contender for the market was the Cross marketed by the O. J. Cross Front Drive Tractor Co of Newark, New Jersey. This design had the engine in the more usual longitudinal position thus making it longer overall than the Christie.

The A & B, which was also in use at the same period, when coupled to a steamer looked more the part than some of its competitors, probably because of spoked wheels as opposed to the steel discs of the Cross and the Christie. However, it was a hybrid — a gasoline-electric, and the two motors were attached to the wheels. These tractors, which also went under the name Hoadley, were marketed by The American and British Mfg Co of Providence, Rhode Island.

Somewhat more unconventional was the three-wheeled Knox-Martin produced by the Knox Automobile Co. This tractor was lengthier than others because the single, front steering wheel was so advanced as to project ahead of the radiator. Indeed, the wheel was so far forward that the steering post cleared the hood and terminated in a gear set above the front wheel. Drive was by way of chains to the rear wheels and a fifth wheel supported the front of the old apparatus.

The bolt-on tractors built by James Boyd & Brother Inc of Philadelphia, Pennsylvania, and the Robinson Fire Apparatus Mfg Co of St Louis, Missouri, were some of the most 'natural-looking' of the conversions, giving the appearance of being designed with the apparatus, and looking much like the front end of normal trucks except for the fact that they carried dual tyres for better adhesion.

By about 1910 the motor vehicle had settled down to a basic layout which was to last a very long time; almost to today, in fact, with changes in detail rather than in fundamentals. The typical fire truck of the period was bonneted, had four wheels, a front-mounted in-line engine, and chemical tanks or pump just behind the driver. It had an open rear body for flaked hose; the ladders hung on the side of the body, and there was a rear step with grab rails. That provided a basic layout which has been little changed.

This was the beginning of a new era in fire equipment, when there would be greater standardisation with the motor truck generally forming the basis for fire apparatus. During the past decade a variety of disparate equipment had been taken into use, often with unsuitable pieces working side by side. Steam appliances continued in operation and manufacture and horses still responded to the fire bells. There was a lot of hard work to fire-fighting but it revolved around just plain fires and rescue – the complications that were to arise from oil and chemical fires, air raids and incendiary attacks, aircraft crashes and motorway accidents were yet to manifest themselves.

The need for experimentation and adaptation continued for much

Below: 1912 Dennis motor pump, formerly in the Clapham Transport Museum.

Bottom: Illustration from a Leyland catalogue shows the open 'Braidwood' style of bodywork of 1911 so popular in the early days.

capital remained tied up in expensive equipment and powerful steam pumps were to stay on the scene for some time, either in their original form or adapted for use with the automobile. The gasoline or petrol engine had been in service for some years, starting as power to pump a horse-drawn outfit. This system found favour chiefly on the continent of Europe, but it was also used in the United States.

The motor vehicle first came to be used in fire departments in the early years of the twentieth century with light models being used to transport fire chiefs, then for light hose-trucks and chemical engines. By 1907, the motor vehicle was becoming accepted. In Germany, Daimler and Bussing chassis were carrying pumps, hoses and ladders. In Britain the Merryweather name was on motor pumps. In France Laffly were building their models and in the United States there were Knox, Waterous, Webb and Seagrave.

Much of the equipment was left over from the horse era, but modified for the new 'motors', and thought was being given to mounting the useful steam boilers and pumps onto the modern motor chassis. For the long-ladder trucks there was the relatively simple solution of removing the front locking carriage and substituting a short motor tractor to bring the equipment up to date quickly. The big and heavy steamers presented a more complicated problem and special two-wheel motor tractors were developed as a result. So, by the second decade motor equipment was taking shape.

In Britain, Dennis Brothers of Guildford in Surrey had produced a series of thirty-, forty-, and fifty-horsepower fire engines on their substantial chassis, the first of which went to the Bradford City Fire Brigade in 1908.

Another name which, like Dennis, has survived was Leyland Motors of Leyland, Lancashire, whose first machine was built in 1909 for delivery to Dublin Fire Brigade in Ireland. In Scotland the Argyll Motor Company of Alexandria-by-Glasgow had started to build fire engines using a Worthington pump; and another Scottish name destined to grace many future fire engines both in Scotland and elsewhere was Halley, who built their first in 1907 and were soon offering three models of twenty-five, thirty-four and forty horsepower. These machines used Mather and Platt pumps.

Henry Simonis of London had made much use of battery-electric chassis for their chemical engines and escape ladders but by now were beginning to offer a little three-wheeled tricar appliance

called the *Liliput* which, with its two-man crew, short ladder, portable fire extinguishers and hand-tools, was known as a 'motor first turnout'. Larger vehicles were built using the Commercar chassis built by Commer Cars of Luton, Bedfordshire.

One of the names not to survive was Lloyd and Plaister of Wood Green, London, who also tried their hand at light vans and taxicabs. The escape carrier they produced was of thirty-five horsepower and speed of 20 mph (32 kph) from a four-cylinder 5 in. × 5 in. (12.7 cm × 12.7 cm) engine with an all-up weight of 3 ton 7 cwt (3,403 kg).

John Morris and Sons of Manchester were using chassis by Belsize Motors, also of Manchester, with pumps by the Pulsometer Engineering Company. Dennis were using the Gwynne pump, while Leyland's offered the Rees Roturbo or Mather and Platt.

In Germany, Adam Opel of Rüsselsheim-am-Main were building fire engines, and so were Hansa-Lloyd of Bremen and Mannesmann-Mulag of Aachen. The famous names of Carl Metz of Karlsruhe, Magirus of Ulm and Daimler of Marienfelde were much to the fore in equipment with many varieties being produced. The MAN (Maschinenfabrik Augsburg-Nurnburg) name appeared on some *feuerwehrfahrzeuge* but they gave up this specialised market to concentrate on commercial truck chassis.

While the European market produced rather plain-looking vehicles equipped as pumps, escape carriers, hose vans, emergency tenders or turntable-ladders, the American product somehow had a more finished appearance with bright colours, crests and flourishes. The American names for various types of apparatus, based on the

'combination' style, seemed more grand and included such equipment as 'combination hose and chemical car'; 'combination pumping and hose engine'; 'dual combination motor pumping engine and hose car'; 'city service hook and ladder truck'; and even 'triple combination pumping chemical and hose car'. On such a vast continent there was room for competition and many manufacturers tried their hand at motor fire equipment.

During the 1910s the Knox Automobile Co of Springfield, Massachusetts, turned out many

Facing page: Circa 1910, USA Mack articulated hook and ladder truck with trailer from an old horse-drawn appliance.

Below: Swiss Saurer of 1914, with Magirus ladder, which remained in service until 1964: now in the Swiss Transport Museum, Lucerne.

engines of various types until they failed towards 1920. Webb Motor Fire Apparatus Co of Vincennes, Indiana, and St Louis, Missouri, produced some interesting equipment notable for being of the cab-over type.

Mack, American La France, Ahrens-Fox, Peter Pirsch, Seagrave, Maxim, Hale, Waterous, White, International Harvester, FWD and Ford were all in production during the second decade of the century

and are still involved in vehicles or equipment today. Some like International Harvester, Ford and White were responsible only for the basic chassis, while the equipment was added by a specialist. Others, such as American La France, Ahrens-Fox, Seagrave and Maxim, built up the complete vehicle although specialist equipment might have been bought from outside.

Small villages and townships

could, perhaps, only afford a Model T Ford with hose-reel, chemical tank, small booster-pump, a short ladder and sundry hand equipment. In larger towns, equipment might run to several pieces by White, Waterous or a small American La France or Seagrave. The larger cities could afford the bigger and more expensive fire trucks and this was the market for the Ahrens-Fox, Seagrave, American La France,

Maxim and Mack fleets.

In addition to the powerful pumpers of 500, 750, 1,000 and 1,200 gal/min (2,273, 3,410, 4,546, 5,455 l/min) there were many smaller ones produced for lesser communities and these were generally of 250, 300, 350 gal/min (1,135, 1,363, 1,590 l/min) capacity. Whereas the small towns generally relied upon a combination pumper with chemical tank, ladders, small-bore hose and regular hose, hand-suctions, hand-extinguishers and small tools, larger towns had additional items such as aerial ladders, a water-tower, a special salvage truck and perhaps a squad car or hose-wagon or turret truck.

In the 1910s, the conversion of older horse-drawn or steam vehicles that had followed the adoption of petrol engines was still going on and there was the paradoxical situation where some large cities were getting their old steamers converted to motor traction while Ahrens-Fox were still building new steamers for anyone who wanted them.

Towards the end of the decade Mack entered the field by producing their own pumper and

Below: Model T Ford fire engine typical of the type used by small towns and villages during the period 1908-27.

the name Stutz appeared as a producer of fire apparatus. The market for electrically propelled vehicles was coming to an end, as fire chiefs realised that the motor chassis was becoming progressively more reliable and the electrics were limited in speed and distance.

By the 1920s some fire apparatus builders, seeing that most of the big cities had been re-equipped with modern motor apparatus, turned their attention to the smaller communities and started turning out pumpers of 350 gal/min (1,590 l/min) — first-quality apparatus which did not swamp the market where there was plenty of room for builders like Prospect and Northern, Oberchain-Boyer, Howe, Childs and Buffalo who used medium-weight truck chassis as the basis for their equipment.

Another boost for the lower end of the market came in the middle 1920s when the American Steam Pump Co introduced the Barton Portable Pump — usually referred to as the Barton front-mounted pump because of its ability to be attached to the front end of the engine crankshaft of many small truck chassis. With this little 200–250 gal/min (909–1,135 l/min) centrifugal pump hundreds of small towns and villages were able to have their own fire truck, at least as a first line of defence.

However, the increasing number of automobiles and trucks in general use was to cause anxiety over the resulting growth of oil and petrol fires. The solution came from the Foamite-Childs Corporation who built a special foam-engine consisting of a large water-tank with foam-making equipment and large hose-reel.

Also in the 1920s the Foamite-Childs Corporation, jointly with the Indian Motorcycle Co, produced

Top: Leyland/BSA motorcycle combination lightweight fire engine of 1926.

Right: Foward-mounted American style aerial ladder clearly demonstrated on a 1910 machine for Allentown, Pennsylvania.

a motorcycle and sidecar outfit. This little machine occupied a space of only 8 ft × 4 ft (2.45 m × 1.20 m), carried 100 ft (30 m) of hose, 25 gal (113 l) of foam, and small foam, soda-acid and CTC extinguishers. Based on a two-cylinder machine and carrying a crew of two, the motorcycle combination was capable of 65 mph (104 kph). Its chief function was as a quickly turned-out apparatus to tackle grass, chimney, trolley-car and automobile fires.

The American fire apparatus market was dominated by home-built equipment, but an interesting development occurred when the German aerial ladder builders Magirus sold some of their ladders in the USA. For some reason, aerial ladders were made with the base of the ladder mounted at the front. In horse-drawn days, this had put the bottom of the ladder just above the fifth wheel of the forecarriage and it remained there into the age of the motor truck – quite sensibly, in fact, because it meant that the base of the weight was then borne by the back axle of the motor tractor. However, with a rigid fire-truck chassis, as opposed to the articulated version, this practice did not hold good; for the base of the ladder was now about midway between the front and rear axles, the point of maximum bending if such a thing did occur.

European style aerial ladders had always been built with the base over the rear axle, even in horse-drawn days. Doubtlessly, because of the confined streets of the old towns of Europe, all ladders had

Top: The Tilling-Stevens petrol-electric chassis had an electrical generator that could power a searchlight and other important devices.

Centre: American Clydesdale truck with bodywork and equipment by Oberchain-Boyer for the Clyde Fire Department, circa 1921.

Left: Ahrens-Fox piston pumper of 1928, one of the most popular with North American fire departments.

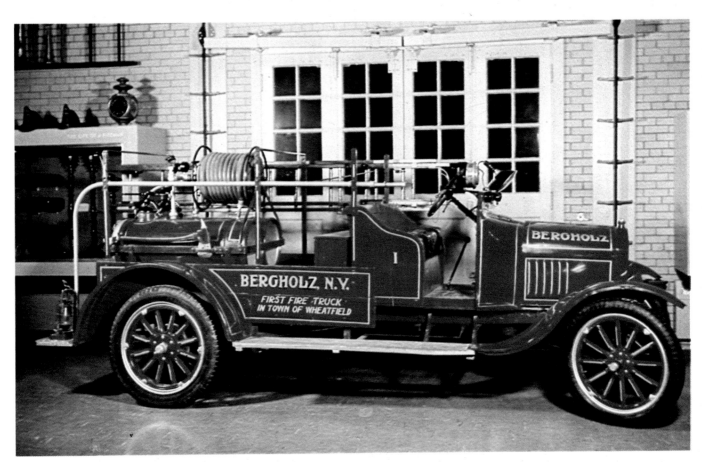

been built very compactly — closing down to about 33 to 36 ft (10–11 m). When the change to motor apparatus took place the old articulated horse-drawn ladders were not adapted to motor tractors as had happened in the United States. Instead, the ladder complete had been transferred to a new motor chassis, and the ladder base placed over the rear axle. But, the European style of ladder did not meet with much approval for about forty years,

when, in the 1960s, rear-mounted aerials and hydraulic platforms made some headway — although during the intervening period the occasional European ladder did make an appearance on the North American continent.

Besides the foam tankers mentioned earlier, other specialised vehicles introduced at this time included smoke extractors, consisting of powerful fans connected to large-diameter flexible hose that was carried into

the building, and special trucks equipped with a number of powerful searchlights. The lights could either be left in situ on the vehicle or positioned closer to the building on the ground or mounted on tripods. A large electric dynamo was powered by the truck's engine or a separate power unit was mounted on the truck. Several reels of cable were also carried so that the lights could be set up some distance from the generating truck.

Above, left: Ford Model T chemical engine, at present on display at the American Museum of Fire Fighting.

Below, left: Gwynne light fire engine for industrial and rural use, based on the maker's 8hp light-car chassis.

Right: Very rare 1940 General Motors (GMC) truck still in use in 1974.

Below: A Studebaker of 1954 with front-mounted pump and twin booster reels.

THE STREAMLINED ERA

A long time passed before fire appliances which carried a crew were equipped to protect the men themselves as they hurried to a blaze. Horse-drawn vehicles were necessarily high off the ground because of the large carriage-type wheels; and the greater the amount of equipment they carried, the more they were inclined to overturn.

The early dirt roads provided some adhesion for the narrow iron-shod wheels of the fire appliance, but granite sets and other forms of metalled road surface, made slippery by a mere shower of rain, could cause galloping horses and their swaying hose-cart or ladder-truck to skid

out of control. There was always a pretty fine line between speedy safe arrival at a fire and a mishap en route. The driver and his crew were constantly fighting a battle to stay on the machine as they hurried along, and the threat to the men of being thrown off if the appliance skidded was ever present. Mechanically propelled vehicles brought little improvement, except that some were slower!
In Europe, crews were still perched on narrow seats either across the body or along the sides of vehicles; in North America they usually stood.

Early self-propelled machines were often older horse equipment modified, and in many cases the

wheels were not changed. Even rubber tyres — which were considerably better than the iron types used previously — were still narrow and could easily slide on wet wooden pavements. Some early conversions were built on motorised chassis and necessitated the use of stronger wooden or iron wheels with rubber tyres of much larger section. For particularly heavy vehicles dual rear wheels were fitted, as on today's vehicles, while the interesting four-wheel-drive

Below: This 1932 Leyland 'Cub' model KSX, with crew seated inside the body, has removable tracks over the rear wheels for negotiating soft ground.

Couple-Gear tractors used with converted horse equipment favoured dual tyres all round.

Heavy steam fire engines were especially difficult to control at speed, particularly if they slid on a slippery surface or a steeply cambered street — a possibility that was not lessened by the smooth profile of the solid rubber tyres. Several different remedies were tried: metal strakes or bars fitted across the tyres; metal studs screwed into the tyres; and metal studded leather gaiters clipped around the tyre were some. Steel chains around the tyres, and the steel studs, were so successful that they are still widely used in bad weather today.

Vehicles could be made much safer, but there still remained the problem of protecting crews. When crew-carrying vehicles were first taken into use the crews accepted some danger during movement as part of the job. But, as speed and the complexity of equipment advanced there seemed to be little change of attitude to crews on the part of designers. In fact, indifference was only apparent. Behind the scenes much thought was being given to increased safety and general protection for crews; although nobody questioned the fact that fire-fighting called for physically tough, courageous and resilient men.

The first, simple improvement was to provide a windshield; but this affected only the forward-facing driver and the officer sitting next to him. During the 1920s, when most fire departments spurned even a windshield, the first fully enclosed cabs were designed for fire truck chassis — but few fire brigades showed any interest. Old traditions die hard, and many fire chiefs considered such a luxury unnecessary for short journeys and argued that they wanted nothing like an enclosed cab that could impede the crew. However, public opinion and a growing number of firemen were hardening against the old open 'pneumonia wagon' which was as great a hazard against health as against safety. Nevertheless, some cabbed vehicles entered the fire service, although for some years they were mainly auxiliary appliances and not first-call apparatus. Some vehicles were more concerned with salvage operations rather than with fire-fighting and they were often based on standard truck chassis suitably modified. They usually carried short extension ladders, ropes, sheets and other implements, and by the addition of a trailer-pump or detachable pump could be used as a combat unit if required.

In North America and continental Europe crews had for a long time been carried to fires in special vehicles, rather than on pump or ladder trucks, which were fitted with varying seating arrangements. Smaller vehicles were similar to touring cars and had cross-bench seats, with or without side doors. Larger vehicles were arranged in

Below: German appliance of the early 1930s with the crew placed inside the body and protected from ejection.

5758

the same manner or had seats facing outwards; or, occasionally, slanted at an angle of forty-five degrees. In North America there was also a trend to put the men in the open rear part of fire appliances in much the same way as was the practice with police wagons.

The American style of patrol wagon gave the crew considerable safety as there was little likelihood of the passengers being thrown out unless the vehicle overturned completely. There was also more comfort, especially if the sides were high and, as sometimes happened, a canvas hood was erected on the grab handles. On the continent of Europe the angled seat or cross-bench design was favoured. Sometimes there were several rows of transverse seats each with its own half-height door, which gave an appearance not unlike that of a British charabanc of the 1920s.

In 1929 British fire-fighters and the people who made their equipment were given cause to think when a driver of the Glasgow brigade produced a design for a wholly enclosed, rigid, six-wheeled vehicle with the appearance of a bus. Variously called a 'New World body' or an 'all-weather pump', the design aroused much interest but two years were to pass before the first enclosed vehicle appeared. While this was happening, a new type of machine was advertised by Dennis Brothers. This machine, designed by the chief officer of the Birmingham brigade, was mounted on a forward-control, low-loading type of chassis and had inside seating for the crew to sit facing inwards.

The next important development came early in 1931 when, almost

Top: American GMC watertender of the 1940s is typical of the enclosed appliance of that era.

Centre: A 1941 Chevrolet shows how the American style of enclosed apparatus used the truck manufacturer's cab.

Bottom: Streamlining on this Austin vehicle is quite pleasing, especially the sweep of the rear end.

simultaneously, Merryweather's built a completely enclosed machine for Edinburgh and Dennis's produced an enclosed appliance for Darlington. The Merryweather had its pumps just behind the driver's seat with the suction inlet at the offside rear of the body and outlets on either side. In contrast, the Dennis machine had the pump so far to the rear that it was outside the enclosed bodywork. While this meant that the pump was excellently accessible for working, it meant too that only a narrow doorway was left to the rear of the back wheels. However, some firemen preferred this layout to the arrangement of having the pump at the rear in the centre of an open-backed body as became the practice in some later enclosed appliances.

Although older appliances, with their open layout and clanging bells and men hanging on for life as they struggled to get into their gear, were excitingly spectacular as they sped along, the new enclosed appliance was no less attractive. It was, too, safer, and as it became more familiar objections to it were forgotten. There was, of course, much discussion about the ideal layout – where the pump and its controls should be mounted; where the suctions should be placed; where portable equipment should be stowed; how wide the doors should be, and so on. An enclosed body provided greater locker space, but that meant urgent training of men in finding any item of equipment without delay – there's no time for searching for keys or fumbling for spanners at a blaze at night. That was a problem that was made no easier by the variety

Top: A later, fully enclosed machine in Holland with rear-mounted pump behind the shutter and hosereel which must be detached before pumping can start.

Centre: A post-war Leyland 'Comet' with bodywork by Campion.

Bottom: A 1958 International pump in service at Oostende, Belgium.

of equipment, for with many small brigades buying just one machine, and not expecting to order another for many years, there was no attempt at standardisation among the many builders of vehicles.

In continental Europe the enclosed appliance appeared early. In 1910 there was a German-built machine that outwardly resembled a large delivery van of the time which was not truly an enclosed appliance as it had no windscreen and could carry a crew of only three. But, it had a pump below the floor, the usual large detachable hose-reels, and a full range of equipment stowed away in several lockers. Moreover, extra appointments could be carried on the roof which was reached by means of a fixed ladder.

An almost identical vehicle, but this time with a windscreen, was produced in 1920, and a year later Magirus built a neat little appliance which featured a completely enclosed cab for the crew. Behind the cab the half-height body was surrounded by a canvas sheet which covered the equipment; and, extremely advanced for the period, the 1½ ton (1,524 kg) capacity vehicle was fitted with pneumatic tyres.

The fire vehicles of continental Europe and Britain of the early 1920s were not dissimilar in appearance, especially in their same open layout. In the middle 1920s German bodywork builders began to change their designs and to pay more attention to the needs of crews, particularly with enclosure. Some styles had cross-bench seating and half-height doors; others had inward-facing seats and the type of rear entrance that was later adopted in Britain and became known as the New World style. In another design the half-height bodywork enclosed seats that faced forwards, backwards and outwards, with access via a side hinged door. The resulting chaos when ten burly firemen tried a quick *eingang* tickles the imagination.

Then, in the 1930s there came

Left: London Fire Brigade style of streamlined appliance on a Dennis chassis, with pump at the rear.

Above: Danish treatment of the fully enclosed body: a 1942 Triangel turntable-ladder for Odense.

Overleaf: A Leyland of the 1930s at a 1969 rally.

the streamline era, with almost everybody trying to make almost everything 'modern' in appearance by curved surfaces, rounded corners, sweeping lines and a shroud for anything that might be thought unsightly. Railway locomotives and trains became shaped like bullets or wedges almost overnight; motor cars took on acutely sloping windshields and raked body pillars; and the domestic electric iron was shrouded in smooth plastic to reduce wind resistance and help high propulsion!

At the same time, the fully enclosed appliance was adopted almost completely by the majority of German and other European producers. The machines built by Magirus and Mercedes Benz were exported to all parts of the world and played a notable part in establishing Germany as a leading manufacturing nation in the world of fire-fighting. Most of the vehicles, except those which carried large hose-reels or ladders, were fully enclosed, and even the exceptions had fully covered compartments for the crew. Many of the turntable-ladders had comfortable enclosed cabs; and some a double cab for greater capacity. But, airfield crash tenders continued to be open in style until the late 1930s; possibly because high-sided vehicles were not appropriate to airfields; because the absence of a roof gave better visibility, and perhaps because the vehicles had also to be used for other duties.

The Germans advanced beyond many countries in their adoption of enclosure, but they did not fall to the blandishments of streamlining as designers had in Britain. Perhaps the Teutonic eye was not attracted to flowing lines or, more probably, perhaps the Germans were more concerned with efficiency than appearance. That is not to say that German products were all corners and ungainly. On the contrary, some of

the machines built in Ulm,
Karlsruhe and Gaggenau were
extremely well designed and
pleasing in appearance: they gave
the impression of being both
complete and efficient.

In the United States the
streamlined appliance was never as
popular as in Britain. Some
vehicles, in 1934, had enclosed
cabs, and in 1935 the machine that
is generally recognised as the
first enclosed fire engine in the
country was acquired by the Fire
Department of Charlotte, North
Carolina. It was a wholly enclosed
Mack with a 750 gal/min
(3,400 l/min) pump and was
known as the Mack Sedan.

In time, the sedan-style
apparatus appeared in greater
numbers, but not in a quantity to
compare with open machines.
Peter Pirsch & Sons built their
first model in 1936, and in the

**Top, left: An American Seagrave
enclosed apparatus of 1940.**

**Centre, left: Probably one of the
first totally enclosed pumps: a Dennis
machine for Edinburgh, 1931.**

**Bottom, left: American Oren-
equipped Ford fitted with truck cab.**

same year Seagrave produced their Safety Sedan. American La France's first model was the Protector with a 600 gal/min (2,727 l/min) pump. Ahrens-Fox started turning out pumpers with enclosed cabs from about 1937, and at the same time the General Fire Truck Corporation built a chassis with a 600 gal/min (2,727 l/min) pump, and, for the comfort of the crew, a complete Ford coupé body. The normal open hose-bed was placed behind the contoured tail of the car.

Another style of the period was an enclosed city-service ladder-truck with a crew cab and four doors by American La France. Seen in Waterloo, Iowa, in 1937, it looked very much like a tanker from the side, being completely enclosed except for access to the ladders at the rear.

General of Detroit built an

Top, right: Powerful 1,000 gallon per minute Ahrens-Fox of New York Fire Department.

Centre, right: Leyland 'Cub' FK9 for Hinckley of 1940.

Below and bottom, right: Last of the pre-war streamliners: two views of a Leyland SFKT2 for Croydon — unlettered because of wartime restrictions.

interesting pump (500 gal/min; 2,273 l/min) in 1937 which was based on a Federal chassis with a semi-forward control cab or cab-over-engine design, and produced a batch of them in 1939 using the recent Ford cab-over-engine chassis. In 1940 American La France produced their new cab-over designs, but there was no rush to adopt this advanced type and, except for apparatus built on production cab-over designs, most builders and fire departments kept stubbornly to the conventional style.

After the Second World War, American La France were first, in 1947, with a design which featured a cab-ahead-of-engine layout for which, because of continuing unwillingness to adopt closed design, the cab could be either open or closed. In the 'fifties other builders turned out both closed cabs and cab-forward designs, but the conventional model was still the favourite and the open cab was preferred to the closed type.

The streamlined era was over. Van-style pumpers were rarely built, although the basic design of fully enclosed bodies was ideal for the growing fleets of heavy rescue trucks. Greater numbers of cab-forward and enclosed cab apparatus were to be seen on the roads in the 1960s, but even today Ford, International, GMC, Chevrolet, Dodge and others include conventional engine layout in their production.

Above, left: Still in service with the Dorset brigade in 1966, a Leyland enclosed machine of the 1930s.

Below, left: A Dodge pump of the 1950s in service at Copenhagen.

Top, right: A 1972 view of the Leyland appliance shown in new condition on page 49.

Centre, right: Fiat pump of the 1950s in service at Rimini.

Bottom, right: Magirus turntable-ladder with crew cab in service at Eindhoven, 1972.

THE WAR AND AFTER

In 1937 the British Government issued a memorandum concerning the organisation of emergency fire brigades in time of war. An announcement was also made that 200,000 auxiliary firemen were required to train and be prepared for any emergency, and that the Government would be issuing pumps and other equipment to fire brigades so that they had more equipment than they normally kept in peacetime.

The fire brigades, who had apparently been expecting bright red pumps and escapes similar to their regular equipment, received either trailer-pumps or self-contained pumping units with an engine attached ready to be bolted to the floor of a general-purpose lorry. They did not view the Government's issue with great favour.

Slowly the Auxiliary Fire Service (AFS, as it became widely and affectionately known) took shape as volunteers joined — albeit in no more than a trickle until the Munich 'crisis' gave impetus to recruitment and preparations for war were put in hand. By early 1939 the AFS had reached the halfway stage in its organisation. Recruitment and the issue of equipment were accelerated, but there were problems over the supply of hose, hose couplings, branches, nozzles, hydrants and, not least, water.

Britain had ignored the example of continental Europe and had failed to standardise the equipment and fittings used by the different fire brigades in the country. Many items were not interchangeable — even with hoses some brigades used instantaneous hose couplings, while others preferred screw-thread couplings. There was a danger that because of variety an AFS appliance called to an emergency could not be coupled to the hoses of the regular peacetime brigade. Such were the problems that attended the development of the AFS and preparation for war.

Much thought had to be given to water supplies. Arrangements were made for sheet-steel dams to be set up on open ground or in the streets of towns. Portable canvas dams that could be braced by steel frames were constructed and placed on open lorries for use with a trailer-pump. These mobile dams proved to be invaluable in ferrying water from rivers and canals to regular pumping units.

Thankfully, when war came the expected heavy air attacks did not occur for a year. Twelve immensely important months provided a precious opportunity for training, equipping and examination of the organisation of the AFS that was well taken.

When, in September 1940, London and the south-east of England were attacked from the air the targets were mainly industrial, with docks being especially severely hit. Soon, streets covered with entwined hoses as pumps from nearby regular and AFS units fought to control fire became a familiar scene, and a threat to the supply of water. Docks, of course, had their own in-built water supply, but many other places did not and their situation became grave when water-mains were ruptured by bombs and firemen stood by, helpless. Bringing water long distances by mobile dams, or using hose-laying lorries and intermediate pumps, worked very well if the streets were free of debris and the hoses were not cut or an obstacle. Street dams helped, too, but their capacity of 5,000 gallons (22,700 litres) was woefully insufficient in long air

raids when enormously fierce fires ensued. The great raid on Coventry in November 1940, and similar raids on other towns, showed how in an air raid any fire more than a short distance from a river or canal was likely to get out of control.

An improvement was made by laying large steel supply pipes in streets on the surface where, if they were damaged, they could be repaired without too much trouble. Another expedient was to make the basements of bombed buildings watertight and fill them with water to provide a standing supply. Similar dams were built where buildings had been utterly demolished.

Fuel, too, could raise difficulties when, for example, a group of pumps were cut off from their supply by falling masonry that had blocked surrounding roads. Many a time the service was kept going by men carrying cans of fuel from a mobile but distant supply.

Maintenance of vehicles and pumps, also, became a problem as air raids kept them in use day after day without respite. Another predicament was caused by the variety of vehicles used to tow trailer-pumps, for all kinds of lorries, large cars and taxicabs were conscripted. The plight of storekeepers who had to try to find spare parts for a motley fleet of British and American saloon cars from stores stocked only with the components required by a regular fire brigade brought matters to a head. The Home Office responded by creating a fleet of Austin vans that they designated Auxiliary Towing Vehicles and

Left: Vehicles with canvas water dams and trailer pumps prepare to move off from Portsmouth.

Top, right: Demonstration of wartime emergency equipment outside County Hall, London, in 1939.

Centre, right: Wartime Ford auxiliary towing vehicle and Dennis trailer pump.

Bottom, right: Austin pumping unit with Tangye pump at the body-builder's prior to delivery.

which were large enough to have benches for the crew and lockers for hose, branches, couplings and tools.

Other vehicles used during the war in Britain included a miniature wheelbarrow-pump which was a tiny centrifugal pump driven by a single-cylinder petrol engine and capable of pumping about 45 gal/min (200 l/min). It had a single front wheel and a pair of handles, just as its name suggests.

Following are details of the more conventional fire-fighting appliances used in Britain during the war:

Light trailer-pump

Output: 140–175 gal/min (636–800 l/min) from a single- or two-stage centrifugal pump powered by a two- or four-cylinder petrol engine of six to eight horsepower. Mounted on a two-wheel trailer-chassis capable of being towed by a medium-power car, and stabilised by legs

when pumping. The pump and engine unit were detachable and fitted with carrying handles.

Pump suppliers: Beresford, Coventry-Climax, Dennis, Forest Protection, Gwynne, Pyrene, Sigmund, Worthington-Simpson.

Engine suppliers: Austin, Coventry-Climax, J. A. P., Jowett, Standard, Morris, Ford.

Medium trailer-pump

Output: 230–320 gal/min (1,045–1,454 l/min) from a single-stage centrifugal pump powered by a ten- to twelve-horsepower four-cylinder petrol engine. Mounted on a two-wheel trailer-chassis for towing by a large car or lorry and stabilised by legs when pumping. Some pump units were detachable.

Pump suppliers: Sulzer, Worthington-Simpson.

Engine suppliers: Ford, Standard.

Large trailer-pump

Top, left: Coventry Climax trailer pump on show at a fire engine rally.

Top, right: 1939 Bedford pump unit in authentic wartime silver-grey colour.

Above, left: Wartime Austin auxiliary towing vehicle in post-war use with the Eastbourne Fire Brigade.

Above, right: Ford 7V wartime pumping unit in action – probably at Ford's Dagenham plant.

Right: Recruiting poster appeals for volunteers to join the British Auxiliary Fire Service immediately before the war.

Output: 430–500 gal/min (1,954–2,273 l/min) from a single- or two-stage centrifugal pump driven by a four- or eight-cylinder petrol engine of fifteen to thirty horsepower. Mounted on a two-wheel trailer-chassis and designed for being towed by a lorry or regular fire engine; not detachable from the chassis.

Pump suppliers: Apex, Beresford, Coventry-Climax, Dennis, Harland,

AUXILIARY
FIRE SERVICE
AFS
LONDON
NEEDS
AUXILIARY FIREMEN
NOW
FRANK
NEWBOULD
ENROL AT ANY FIRE STATION
CIVIL DEFENCE

Kerr, Pyrene, Scammell.

Engine suppliers: Ford, Dennis, Coventry-Climax, Meadows, Scammell.

Heavy pump

A single- or two-stage centrifugal pump driven by a petrol engine of about thirty horsepower and mounted to a frame for bolting to the floor of a lorry or four-wheel trailer, or as required.

Pump suppliers: Gwynne, Sulzer, Tangye.

Engine suppliers: Leyland, Ford.

Self-propelled heavy unit

A standard production 2–3 ton (2,032–3,048 kg) lorry-chassis fitted with a cab, crew compartment, lockers for hose and other equipment, and a roof gantry for ladders. A heavy pump unit with its own engine was bolted to the rear of the body.

Vehicle suppliers: Austin, Bedford, Ford, Morris.

Pump suppliers: Gwynne, Sulzer, Tangye.

Engine suppliers: Leyland, Ford.

Extra-heavy pump

A single-stage centrifugal pump driven by a six-cylinder forty-nine-horsepower petrol engine as a self-contained unit and mounted on a standard production lorry-chassis with a cab, crew compartment, ladder gantry, and side lockers.

Pump suppliers: Gwynne.

Engine suppliers: Leyland.

Chassis suppliers: Austin or Bedford.

Auxiliary towing vehicle

A 2 ton (2,032 kg) production lorry-chassis fitted with a cab and integral van body with seats for the crew and internal lockers for hose and small equipment. Designed to tow a large trailer-pump.

Vehicle suppliers: Austin.

Escape carrier

A 4–6 ton (4,064–6,096 kg) standard lorry-chassis with enclosed cab and crew compartment, lockers for loose equipment and an attachment for carrying a detachable wheeled escape. Mounted amidships: a 130 gal (590 l) water-tank, two 120 ft (36.5 m) hose-reels of $\frac{3}{4}$ in. (20 mm) hose, and a engine-driven 20 gal/min (91 l/min) pump with connections for hydrants. A tow-bar was fitted for towing a trailer-pump. Some vehicles were fitted with a front-mounted Barton 300 gal/min (1,363 l/min) centrifugal pump.

Chassis suppliers: Austin, Ford.

Escape suppliers: Bayley, Merryweather, Morris, Youngman.

Turntable-ladder (1)

A 100 ft (30 m) four-section, mechanically operated, steel ladder mounted on a special heavy-duty long chassis equipped with enclosed cab, a locker for loose equipment and outrigger screw jacks for stability.

Ladder suppliers: Merryweather.

Chassis suppliers: Leyland.

Turntable-ladder (2)

A 60 ft (18 m) three-section, manually operated, steel ladder mounted on a 4–6 ton (4,064–6,096 kg) lorry-chassis equipped with an enclosed cab and crew compartment, lockers for small tools and outrigger screw jacks for stability.

Hose-laying lorry

A standard production 5 ton

discharge off the sloping tail-board as the vehicle was driven forward.

Chassis suppliers: Ford.

Mobile dam

A standard lorry with flat or sided body carrying a canvas water container kept rigid by an internal tubular steel framework. Normal capacity: 500 gal (2,270 l) or 1,000 gal (4,546 l). Other types of dams were rigid steel enclosed tanks, or formed from collapsible steel sheets. The dams were often used with a demountable pump or a trailer-pump.

Pipe carrier

An articulated lorry of 6–8 ton (6,096–8,128 kg) capacity with a stake-sided trailer for carrying lengths of rigid steel piping.

Special appliances

Several other types of vehicles were built for special purposes, but not

capacity of 220 gal/min (1,000 l/min) or 175 gal/min (800 l/min) and were powered by a four-cylinder four-stroke engine of about twenty-seven horsepower or a two-cylinder two-stroke engine of similar power. A light portable pump, for use in rural areas, had an output of 175 gal/min (800 l/min) and was powered by a fifteen brake-horsepower two-stroke engine.

Fire equipment in Germany had been standardised for some years, so there was no confusion over incompatible components. Even in general design and layout German appliances were made to similar specifications and there was little deviation between different manufacturers. An enormous advantage resulted when crews had to be trained quickly and had to learn their way about only a few machines.

Basic appliances were made in Germany by Bussing, Henschel,

Left: Fordson 7V escape carrier with front-mounted Barton pump.

Above, left: Austin auxiliary towing vehicle (ATV) with Dennis trailer pump.

Above, right: Early 1940s Klockner-Deutz LF15-type and fireman with hose-carrier on his back.

(5,080 kg) lorry-chassis with enclosed bodywork and cab. Interior of body arranged to accommodate approximately 600 ft (182 m) of ready-connected hose laid in flaked fashion for easy

in such quantities as those listed above. These special appliances included: mobile kitchens, breakdown lorries, mobile canteens, telephone vans, control units, petrol tankers, water tankers, repair vans, emergency tenders, salvage tenders and foam tenders.

In Germany measures for dealing with air attacks included an increase in small appliances such as trailer-pumps and demountable pumps, both of which had been much used in the peacetime fire service. The trailer-pumps had a

Magirus and Mercedes with a six-cylinder diesel engine of 110 bhp and with an Amal-Hilpert, Magirus or Metz front-mounted two-stage centrifugal pump. Output was about 550 gal/min (2,500 l/min) and there were three deliveries on each side. Metz, anticipating incendiary attacks, made an extremely portable pump which could be carried on a man's back and used quickly on small fires in difficult places. Another wartime measure was to equip each turntable-ladder with a bicycle for speedy

Women! You are needed in

THE NATIONAL
FIRE SERVICE
AS FULL-TIME OR PART-TIME MEMBERS

You can train to be a telephonist, despatch rider, driver, canteen worker and for many other duties.

APPLY FOR PARTICULARS TO NEAREST FIRE STATION OR EMPLOYMENT EXCHANGE

Printed for H.M. Stationery Office by Geo. Gibbons Ltd. 51-2219

communications if other means failed.

In 1938 the Germans matched the British in planning wartime fire services. Arrangements were made to produce a series of standard fire trucks which included light, medium and heavy pumpers and a series of turntable-ladders of 55 ft (17 m), 72 ft (22 m) and 105 ft (32 m) sizes. As experience of wartime precautions grew other types of vehicles were developed for special purposes, such as for service with the Luftwaffe.

The following table gives a general description of the type of equipment built for wartime use:

Production of the wartime appliances was in the hands of famous German builders of chassis and fire equipment. Chassis builders included Daimler-Benz, Klockner-Humbolt-Deutz and Opel, and bodywork and equipment came from Magirus, Metz, Fischer, Flader, Hoenig, Koebe, Mayer-Hagen and Rosenbauer, the last being an Austrian firm.

The war over, the fire service had to recover from a break of six years in normal operating practices. But there was no question, certainly in Britain, of merely returning to the conditions of 1939.

Some of the pre-war builders of fire appliances had disappeared and others did not renew their activities in the field. There was, too, a quite distinct change of style when production got under way.

Among the notable absentees from the ranks of regular manufacturers were Leyland's who, although their appliances before the war had been popular, and attractive, decided to concentrate on goods vehicles and buses, and on exporting. However, they did not entirely abandon fire-fighting. A few fire engines were built on the Comet chassis, but men who operated them thought that they

Pumps	LF8	1½–2 ton (1,524–2,032 kg) chassis with 1,400 gal/min (800 l/min) pump
	LF15	3 ton (3,048 kg) chassis with 2,640 gal/min (1,500 l/min) pump
	LF25	4¼ ton (4,572 kg) chassis with 3,400 gal/min 2,500 l/min) pump
Turntable-ladders	DL17	1½ ton (1,524 kg) chassis with 55 ft (17 m) ladder
	DL22	3–4¼ ton (3,048–4,572 kg) chassis with 72 ft (22 m) ladder
	DL32	4¼ ton (4,572 kg) chassis with 105 ft (32 m) ladder
	DL36	4¼ ton (4,572 kg) chassis with 118 ft (36 m) ladder
Foam-trucks	S3	3 ton (3,048 kg) chassis with tanks and foam-making equipment
	S4.5	4¼ ton (4,572 kg) chassis with tanks and foam-making equipment
Tank-pumpers	TLF15	3 ton (3,048 kg) chassis with 2,640 gal/min (1,500 l/min) pump
	TLF25	4¼ ton (4,572 kg) chassis with 3,400 gal/min (2,500 l/min) pump

Facing page: British poster urges women to join the National Fire Service in support capacities and so release men for active military service.

Below: Mercedes-Benz L4500 with Magirus bodywork supplied to the Luftwaffe around 1941.

were too tall and narrow. There was also the Firemaster, based on the Worldmaster bus-chassis, which was available for a time from 1958 but with no noticeable success. Other Leyland and Leyland-Albion chassis have been used for fire appliances, but most of these have been built in small quantities for export.

Dennis Brothers returned to peacetime anxious to improve on their former position in the market and they soon produced a range of vehicles to support their efforts. Since the early days of motor appliances Dennis had produced quality pumps and other equipment, and had sometimes provided chassis for other manufacturers' turntable-ladders – a field in which at the time they were not dominant. Although Dennis's had a good fire engine business they were also producing good-quality truck-chassis, and they had wartime commitments to build fire vehicles and trailer-pumps still to fulfil. Eventually they turned to a new fire-chassis and started their production with a bonneted series that featured either an open cab or a truck cab. Dennis's, too, built their own engines, but the introduction of the Rolls-Royce petrol engine into fire vehicles was an important advance and the engine was soon the standard power unit. The Dennis range of equipment was made complete when the company acquired the British franchise for the German Metz turntable-ladder. This ladder was then, and continued to be in later models, mounted on a forward-control chassis.

Merryweather's appliances were originally built on their Albion-Merryweather chassis with normal control, but, after a while, Bedford and Commer chassis were used for lighter vehicles and AEC's chassis for larger equipment. A few vehicles, including some unusual AEC's with turntable-ladders, were supplied with normal control, and there were still orders for the old open Braidwood style of body. In time, the AEC chassis was supplied only fully fronted,

and, as they changed their designs, volume producers started to make forward-control cabs.

Other manufacturers of the period were Pyrene, Miles, Arlington, Whitson, Campion, Carmichael, Hampshire, Haydon, Angus, Sun, Morris, Foamite and Kerr, all of whom used proprietary chassis. Some of these companies had been involved in building fire engines before the war; others, who were new to the market,

entered the field because wartime experience of making heavy armament and aircraft enabled them to apply engineering knowledge and processes to fire equipment that were quite different from conventional methods. New techniques such as metal framing, stress panelling, riveting, and the use of plain metal parts and metal-faced plywood became widely accepted. Up to the late 1930s bodywork had changed little in construction from the ash framing and mahogany panelling of the horse-drawn era. It was built to last perhaps fifty years, and was mounted on chassis which were expected to have similar endurance. However, times were changing. Mass production and increasing legislation concerning road transport meant that to build a vehicle that never wore out was bad economics. An 1846 manual engine might still be in use a

hundred years later, and steam pumps were employed in the Second World War; but modern times called for vehicles that would last for about ten years and then be replaced, and that was the new policy. At the same time, there was

constant research and improvement. When the first post-war appliances were taken into use they put up creditable performances, but each replacement was better. For the previous model to last only about ten years was very convenient when it came to justifying the purchase of something new.

In the second decade of the post-war era the mass-producers secured a larger part of the market. Bedford had been gradually increasing their share since their S type appeared, and their C and TK models extended the process. But they had competitors. Popular chassis came from Commer and Dodge, and when the Ford D appeared it was equally successful. Yet, oddly, the two ends of the market changed very little. At the lower, or smaller, end there was the Land-Rover, and at the upper, or larger end, there was Thornycroft's

Nubian. Both still sell well, although the Range-Rover is gaining on the Land-Rover and the ageing Nubian had to undergo considerable modification to give it a new lease of life.

During this time bodywork design was simplified, jack-knife and sliding doors were tried, plastics gained ground, unpainted panels became fashionable, and rolling shutters were fitted to lockers. Attention was turned, too, to colour and the marking of appliances. For a very long time fire appliances had been painted red in the belief that the colour was strikingly outstanding and associated by most people with danger. However, tests showed that red by itself was not particularly noticeable, especially at night, and it did not mix easily into the self-coloured aluminium that was becoming popular.

Various forms of marking and visible warning were put to the test – blue or amber lights flashed or rotated or held steady, and some vehicles were painted overall in yellow which was expected to stand out more than the familiar red. Unfortunately, British Rail, National Carriers, the Post Office for some of their vehicles, and often local dustcarts, all used a similar colour with the result that a yellow fire engine made little impact.

Experiments with colour have also been made by brigades in Europe. Some vehicles have been painted red and white, and others red with reflective markings and further reflective or vividly contrasting stripes or flashes. In Germany, Wiederhold's fluorescent paint Wiedolux was used in Frankfurt, Hamburg, Cologne and Berlin to paint appliances, sometimes overall and sometimes partly in white on a very bright red. The same experiment was made in Rotterdam.

In the United States apparatus is painted in many more styles than in Europe. The liveries are all white, red and white, yellow and white, dark maroon, all yellow, lime green, and silver grey, just to mention a few. Among the markings and signals there are white lights, yellow lights, red lights, blue lights, flashing lights, rotating lights, Mars lights, Roto-ray lights – think of some device that will attract attention and you will find it in a fire brigade somewhere in the USA. But, there is no attempt to standardise colour, marking, arrangement or intensity of the lights. Some are confused with ordinary street lighting, some give a misleading impression of the size of their vehicle, others have a blinding effect. The result is confusion, and inability among even the best-intentioned general drivers to help a fire appliance go about its business.

In Germany, after the war, the fire-fighting manufacturing industry returned to conditions similar to those of the 1930s. Daimler-Benz, Magirus and Metz reappeared as large manufacturers with Opel, Bussing, Borgward, Ford and Hanomag playing lesser roles. In general, the vehicles that they built were like those produced before the war.

However, in a country that was accustomed to standardisation the authorities were not likely to let progress stagnate. Soon, new standards were drawn up for major appliances and items of equipment. Specifications were issued for each type of appliance, and, to make administrative identification simple, each was given an abbreviated reference taken from its full description :

KW (*Kranwagen*) : a mobile crane ;

RW (*Rustwagen*) : an emergency tender ;

DL (*Drehleiter*) : a turntable-ladder ;

TroTLF (*Trocken-Tankloschfahrzeug*) : a dry-powder tender with water-tank and pump ;

LF (*Loschgruppenfahrzeug*) : a pumper with hose and other equipment and a crew cab ;

and many others. Where, because of size or output, there were variants within types additional figures were used to denote the difference – figures after DL indicated the height of the ladder in metres, and LF8 and LF16 showed the output of the pump in hundreds of litres a minute, e.g. 800 l/min, 1,600 l/min and so on.

Also in Europe there was a trend not to have a vehicle's engine out in front under a hood or bonnet but to adopt the more compact forward-control or cab-over-engine design. In early steam or electric fire trucks the driver was at the very front behind a metal apron and the motive power was somewhere behind him ; but when

the internal combustion engine was taken into use it was put at the front where the driver could control it more easily. Except for a few small vehicles built by AEG and Magirus, this was the style of all German fire trucks up to 1959. Then Mercedes-Benz introduced the *frontlenker*, or cab-over, type of chassis, which was followed by a similar design from Magirus about ten years later. Both companies also continued with the traditional pattern of cab for some time afterwards.

Below, left: Ward La France pumper of 1948.

Below, right: Bedford/Rosenbauer pump at the RAI exhibition at Amsterdam in 1973. A fluorescent paint is used with contrasting stripes on the body.

Bottom, left: Mack 'Model L' pumper of 1951.

Bottom, right: Bedford/HCB-Angus watertender in a 1972 display of modern fire-fighting equipment.

Today's fire-fighting equipment is complicated and intricate but the search continues for even further advanced methods and equipment which can tackle the new hazards caused by modern technology and the rapid pace of change. The materials used to build the places where we live and work, and their services, are constantly changing, and as they do so different dangers arise. In many homes the old open fire has given way to central heating, and there have been fewer chimney fires. However, this improvement has often been offset by fires resulting from the increased use of paraffin heaters that are carelessly handled or inadequately maintained.

Other improvements can lead to risks which are not at first apparent. Cold, whitewashed ceilings are replaced by neat polystyrene tiles which easily melt and burn, especially if painted. The old horsehair sofa has disappeared and in its place there are easy chairs covered with polyvinyl chloride softened by cushions filled with polyurethane chippings which can easily burst into flame if placed too near an open fire and give off poisonous fumes.

The buildings in which we live also change. Little cottages in towns are demolished and in their place mighty blocks of flats tower upwards far above the reach of rescue appliances. Materials used in buildings often cause concern to fire authorities, especially when large areas are covered with sheet-glass or plastics. The glass can shatter and send razor-sharp fragments showering down, and the disastrous fire at the Summerland Amusement Park in the Isle of Man in 1973 showed the folly, not appreciated at the time, of

Below:Fiat/Salvani appliance for the protection of large, high-risk industrial premises. The large roof-mounted monitor gives a rapid discharge of great quantities of foam from a safe distance.

using large spreads of plastic covering.

Down on the farm it used to be the hayrick fire which was commonplace. Nowadays, large-scale intensive farming brings fresh problems. A single fire can destroy equipment worth many thousands of pounds, and large amounts of chemical fertilisers, insecticides and pesticides provide a source of toxic fumes.

The manufacturing industry probably stands the greatest risks. Not only is the value of industrial premises enormously high, but many production processes involve highly complicated machinery which, if damaged or destroyed, takes a long time to be replaced, with consequent loss of production. The demand for artificial substitutes for many rapidly disappearing conventional materials is largely met by products from a petro-chemical base. The result is that many industries are tied to chemicals and chemical processes which have a built-in risk of fire and explosion, and place great danger in the path of rescuers.

In the world of transport progress has manifested itself spectacularly in larger, heavier and faster aircraft, and only the fortunate infrequency of serious accidents has spared airlines and passengers from death-rolls of fearful dimensions. The numbers of vehicles using the roads and their speed have made motorway accidents horrible, and the ever-increasing amounts of acids, chemicals and other hazardous loads carried by hauliers offer the grim prospect of disaster.

The role of the fire-fighting force is changing, too. Originally to

quench fire, then to rescue from fire, it is often today to deal with emergencies where there is not even a wisp of smoke. The modern fire engine is equipped with a vast range of tools and equipment that make the fire-fighters' task bearable, but not easy: cutting tools, lifting gear, resuscitation equipment, portable boats, emergency lighting and much else besides are somewhere to be found in the inventory of the fire department. The increasing amount of dangerous liquids carried in bulk road-tankers are causing fire authorities much alarm over the consequences of accidents involving these vehicles. It is no use saying that the liquids should not travel; movement at great cost would not even be considered if it were not necessary. The trouble is that the place of production and the point of consumption are often far apart and safe transport must be carried out. Yet, cases have been known of drivers being quite ignorant about the nature of their loads. An accident to a tanker carrying a nameless liquid, and possibly a long way from the source, could lead to great confusion and a

Left: Mack 'CF' pumper shows the position of front coupling for hydrant inlet or suction. The pump controls are at both sides of the body.

Below: Calavar Firebird 125 demonstrates its fixed monitor at an oil storage installation.

Bottom: Mercedes-Benz/Metz 6-wheeled SLF on 2626 model chassis for the protection of oil and chemical installations. It carries a rear-mounted pump, roof monitor, water, CO_2 and foam-making equipment.

Overleaf: Hino hydraulic platform turntable-ladder with amidship pump and searchlights, in a typical Nippon setting.

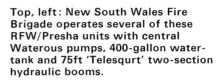

Top, left: New South Wales Fire Brigade operates several of these RFW/Presha units with central Waterous pumps, 400-gallon water-tank and 75ft 'Telesqurt' two-section hydraulic booms.

Centre, left: Magirus pump/water-tanker with roller shutters covering the equipment lockers.

Bottom, left: Mercedes-Benz 2623 6-wheel-drive chassis with pump amidships and large-output roof monitor in service at Zurich airport, 1977.

Below: Mack articulated pumping unit of the New York Fire Department's revolutionary Super Pumper complex. A second Mack unit is used to mount the large-output fixed monitors. Satellite trucks are also used with this giant pumper.

threat to the road, drains, underground services, other traffic and pedestrians.

To meet such a contingency a system known as 'hazchem' has been devised by chemical producers working in collaboration with police and fire authorities. Special coloured plates and codes displayed on the tanker should make it easier for rescue teams quickly to ascertain the nature of the load, its characteristics, the type of antidote necessary if one is needed, storage requirements and the method of handling the material in an emergency.

At least one fire department takes the matter so seriously that it has a large tanker standing by ready to attend tanker accidents. This large tanker contains several compartments, some of which are filled with water for the purpose of extinguishing fire or washing down. The empty compartments are there to take in any liqiud which has to be removed from a crashed vehicle for the sake of safety or recovery.

A fire brigade that is most advanced in its thinking is that of Frankfurt-on-Main in West Germany, where the fire service has worked closely with a number of vehicle and equipment manufacturers to form a finely equipped and efficient service. One of the world's busiest airports in their midst, handling large passenger-carrying and freight aircraft, has caused much thought to be given to airfield emergencies, but not to the exclusion of other risks in the area.

The airport has the largest of the local vehicles – Faun 8 × 8 chassis with bodywork equipment by either Metz, Magirus or Minimax. These powerful machines are capable of traversing the airport and surrounding areas at high speed and dealing a hard blow at a fire upon arrival. With large capacities and high outputs, the appliances can dispense huge amounts of foam or dry powder even when they are a considerable distance from the blazing aircraft so as to make rescue operations

possible. A large tanker is used to lay a carpet of foam on the runway when it is known that an aircraft might have to land with its undercarriage still retracted. This foam carpet has the effect of reducing the risk of fire that could follow from sparks from the skidding aircraft igniting spilled fuel.

Another problem facing fire-fighters on a vast airfield, or even in the surrounding countryside, is the great amount of water or foam required, and the urgency. Modern high-output fire apparatus can exhaust its own supply of water or foam in a matter of a few minutes and it is imperative that there should be a stand-by tanker ready if no hydrant is available. A similar situation can arise when serious fires or spillages occur on national highways and motor

routes where there is often no hydrant system. At Frankfurt, one such vehicle is a modern four-axle articulated tanker with a capacity of 2,640 gallons (12,000 litres).

Today, fire equipment builders are spread out across the world and involved in a variety of sizes and types of businesses ranging from completely State-owned plants in some Socialist regimes to small family concerns in free-enterprise countries. Between those two extremes there exist several hundred makers who cover all the stages of construction, with some units producing such specialist items as pumps or cabs. Another company may build only the bodywork and buy in components that are better made by other professional specialists. Yet another firm may produce literally everything: chassis, cab, body,

Above, right: 1976 LTI 100ft aerial ladder in service at Topeka.

Top, right: Skuteng-equipped 4 x 4 cross-country vehicle in Norway.

Above, left: Magirus RW2 rescue appliance, showing the wide variety of equipment carried on the vehicle.

Top, left: HCB-Angus-equipped rapid intervention vehicle on light Dodge chassis for airport use.

Right: Crown/Maxim 100ft aerial ladder.

pump, ladders, hose, fittings, tools, and so on. Production levels vary widely. Some of the large groups can turn out several hundred appliances in a year; a medium producer might work to the theory that seventy a year is right if he is to retain personal relationships with his clients; and the real custom builder, producing three to five units a year, is happy

because he really is in touch with his customers, perhaps on a daily basis, and he can keep his business as small as he wishes.

Some firms have roots going back well into the manual and steam days and they have managed to adapt to continuing change. Other companies started up in the days of expansion of the motor world and have hung on to their positions through good and bad days, perhaps diversifying to other things when the going is hard. There are also newcomers, perhaps because they are part of another industry and are brought to fire appliances by a new phase in the industry, while others enter the market with fresh ideas and make a niche for themselves.

The ever-changing market keeps the industry alive and on its toes. There is a constant demand

for new ideas and no shortage of agile minds to offer ideas. Every year sees new notions in some facet of the industry – improved hose material, larger output pumps, more powerful rescue tools, a change in pump position, a new control-panel layout, compacter ladder-trucks, better access to equipment, a new extinguisher compound, or further-reach aerial ladders.

The simple ladder is a good subject of research. It was a means of access and rescue many hundreds of years ago and remained almost unaltered until the nineteenth century, when fresh attention was given to rescue from the upper floors of buildings. The extension ladder was the first step away from the straight ladder; then carriage wheels were added to make it more mobile and

turn it into the wheeled escape which found great favour in Britain. To give the long-extension ladder a firm base for rescue purposes the Germans mounted it on a metal-frame bed and placed it on a suitable chassis. As the demand for greater lengths grew the ladders were trussed for strength. Metal sockets were tried, then came steel ladders, mechanical extensions, light alloy ladders, hydraulic control, and lengths of 100 ft, 145 ft, 170 ft and 197 ft (30 m, 44 m, 52 m, 60 m). Then, outside fire-fighting, a company produced a hydraulically controlled, jointed, folding boom with an operator's cage at the top end. Its potential was quickly appreciated and soon brigades all over the world were trying out the new aerial rescue platform and making their own

modifications.

The position of the pump and its controls is another aspect of design which raises problems even after seventy years of motor pumps. Pumps have been placed out in front of the radiator and driven off the front of the engine crankshaft. They have been put approximately in the middle of the vehicle, with outlets and controls on either or both sides. They have been located at the rear of the vehicle. Each of these positions had its advantages and disadvantages, its supporters and its critics. The position of the pump controls had usually been at the pump connections, but not always. More recently there has been a move to transfer the pump controls and pump operator up onto the vehicle away from pump connections. Here, it is argued, he has a better view of both sides of the apparatus and is away from traffic. On large airfield crash tenders the controls are normally in the cab because, as the pumps will often be in operation even before the vehicle has come to rest, an outside control is out of the question, except for the use of side-lines for small tasks.

Many years ago similar arguments raged about the best type of fire-pump. Originally, pumps were of the piston type; then came the rotary style, followed by the centrifugal where the water is taken into the centre of the casing and flung outwards by centrifugal force. There were many advocates, supporters and arguments on all sides, with many tests and ensuing claims put up on behalf of all three types of pump. The centrifugal pump emerged as the most successful, but it is not likely to remain unsupplanted.

Left: New York Fire Department fire boat 'Governor Alfred E. Smith' in action at an oil fire.

Bottom: Mack pumper of New York Fire Department.

Below, right: New York Fire Department's high-expansion foam unit on a Mack cab-over chassis.

Below, left: Calavar Firebird 125 hydraulic platform, mounted on a six-wheel chassis, in the closed travelling position.

Overleaf: Simon Snorkel on a Ford chassis undergoing pre-delivery check prior to going to the Philippines.

AIRCRAFT CRASH TRUCKS

The fire service has developed alongside man's technical advances – as each new achievement has produced its new emergency a fresh counter-measure has been not far behind.

One of the most spectacular advances in the world during the past seventy years has taken place in all forms of transport, but especially in air travel. Almost as soon as the early airplanes started to fly there was a need for motor vehicles to fuel, tow, transport or rescue them; although many developments took place at a time when the motor car was also finding its feet.

The first means of combating an aircraft fire could only have been by hand-held extinguishers, although there was no time to spare with a wood and canvas machine even if only a small fuel-tank was fitted. In all probability some of the first aircraft mishaps were attended by manual fire engines, but it was a Model T Ford that became the first airfield crash tender.

Early crash tenders were merely motor vehicles adapted to carry a number of hand-extinguishers, or a chemical foam-tank and hose-reel, to deal with the size of fire expected. The foam-compound was carried in cylinders containing 30 gal (136 l) and when mixed with water made about eight times that amount of fire-killing foam.

Because the flimsy construction of early aircraft made them very prone to breaking up on impact with the ground the first priority was to rescue the passengers and crew. Even during the 1930s most commercial aircraft were quite small and lightly built by comparison with those of today. Quite often the aircraft's undercarriage would collapse on landing, with the result that the fuselage was near to the ground and needed only short ladders to free the passengers. Even if the undercarriage was intact the passenger compartment could be reached by ladder.

The comparatively small fuel-tanks of early aircraft meant that fire in a crash was much less severe than it is today. Rescue could be

attempted by the crash tender crew and for a while heavy asbestos suits made approach to the aircraft possible, although for only short periods.

During the 1930s the old chemical type of foam was superseded by mechanical foam made on the vehicle by mixing water, foam and air together in a rotor-type pump and discharging it through canvas hose and branch pipes. This type of foam was known as saponine because it derived from soap. Another experiment was to add methyl-bromide to the foam in order to increase its fire-quenching property, but that had the disadvantage of restricting expansion of the foam.

Carbon dioxide (CO_2) was also tried with success, usually to complement the foam on the crash tender although some vehicles used the gas by itself. Because the gas was kept in a compressed liquid state it had to be stored in special steel cylinders, which were heavy. These cylinders were carried in batteries and linked to feed one or two small-bore hose-reels whose hose terminated in a large flat funnel which was directed towards the fire. But, to attack an aircraft fire of any size at close range with a small hand-held extinguisher, or even a CO_2 funnel, was so difficult as to be almost impossible. So, the hoses of foam-pumps were extended by the addition of long metal tubes which ended in a small funnel-shaped mouthpiece and put the fire-fighter a little more than arm's length from the blaze.

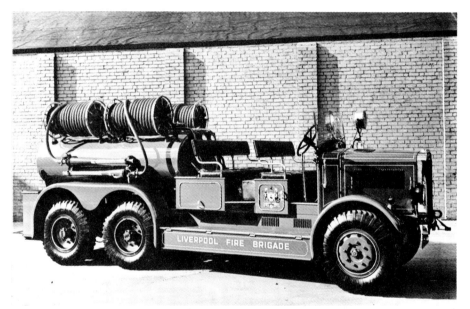

Left: 1935 Bedford airfield appliance built to deal with emergencies to aircraft such as that in the background.

Top, right: This mid-1930s Ford with CO_2 equipment used to tour Britain with a flying circus.

Centre, right: A special Leyland 6-wheel cross-country CO_2-type appliance supplied to Liverpool Speke airport in 1939.

Bottom, right: Bedford airfield crash tender with CO_2 equipment for the Bristol Aeroplane Company; early 1930s.

With the introduction of all-metal aircraft there came a gradual growth in size, passenger capacity and fuel storage, and an increase in risk for which new ways of fighting fire and rescue had to be found. Mechanical foam was replaced by protein foam which had better smothering characteristics. Improvements were made to the delivery pumps on vehicles so that they provided a higher, and therefore quicker, rate of discharge of the vast amount of foam that was required. The unsettled state of European affairs also caused some countries to consider how efficient their fire services would be in war, and to give thoughtful attention to the special vehicles that would be needed to fight fire in airfield buildings as well as in crashed aircraft.

Germany produced some very efficient machines and familiar names — Magirus, Mercedes Benz, Henschel and Opel — were to be found on various designs of vehicles for use at aircraft manufacturing plants and airfields. For cross-country work tyres with large-section treads were used, and some vehicles had six wheels and a large water-tank plus a trailer carrying foam equipment and hose-reels. Some designs were very similar to those used by civilian authorities, even to the trailer being included in complete enclosure. Others favoured the open style of crew compartment with its better aerial view and low profile. Foam was invariably the principal extinguishing medium and ancilliary equipment included long-handled hooks, axes, spades, hand-extinguishers, searchlights and sometimes an extension ladder. Typical of the design of the period was the front-mounted pump which was usually protected by a large, strong bumper.

Appliances at British airfields were somewhat mixed and included many civilian-style engines. Among the pre-war British Royal Air Force types there were adaptations of domestic civilian appliances and some interesting six-wheel conversions of AA and BB Fords and RD Morris Commercials. There were also Crossley six-wheelers which had a remarkable streamlined, fully-enclosed body with a 200 gal (909 l) water-tank, twin air-foam

pumps chain-driven from the vehicle's engine, and four 80 lb (36 kg) CO_2 cylinders. The next style to appear was a similar Crossley 6×4 chassis, but reversed in design with its fully open layout and small windscreen. Its equipment contained a 300 gal (1,363 l) water-tank, 28 gal (127 l) foam liquid and four 60 lb (27 kg) CO_2 cylinders.

Wartime equipment for the Royal Air Force included Crossley 4×4 chassis with canvas top, open cab and 300 gal (1,363 l) water-tank; Fordson WOT 1 6×4 with soft top cab and 400 gal (1,818 l) tank; locally built conversions of American Jeeps as rescue trucks; and later versions of the WOT 1 Ford which embodied a separate Ford V8 engine for powering the

pump and the use of 500 gal (2,273 l) water-tanks as supply trucks for use with the WOT 1 Fords.

Although the United States did not enter the war until December 1941 the country's tremendous manufacturing facilities were already being put to good use as the government saw that the European struggle could spread. At first, civilian equipment was adapted to military design to provide normal open-style pumpers of 750 gal/min (3,400 l/min) capacity.

In fire-fighting, as in other fields of technology, a national emergency such as war accelerates

development, and the great increase in the numbers of aircraft being flown during the Second World War caused much thought to be given to the problems of tackling aircraft disasters. An important advance was the introduction of a bulk CO_2 tanker. This Cardox system, as it was called, consisted of a pressure

Below: This recent Massport Chubb 'Pathfinder' is designed to produce the enormous quantities of foam required to combat emergencies to modern aircraft.

vessel carrying 3 tons (3,048 kg) of liquid CO_2 which was dispensed at low pressure through special booms mounted on the roof and in front of the radiator and controlled from inside the cab. A large-diameter hose-reel was positioned just to the rear of the cab for discharging the CO_2 by hand. A supply of foam was also carried on the vehicle and this could be used by itself or mixed with CO_2.

An early post-war design of airfield crash tender in Britain was the Pyrene foam and CO_2 tender which used either Thornycroft Nubian or Bedford QL chassis, both of which had four-wheel drive. The Nubian was normally powered by a Thornycroft AC4/1 four-cylinder petrol engine, but a more

popular choice was the Rolls-Royce eight-cylinder petrol engine which gave a superior performance. The well-known Bedford QL was the first ex-military type to be used as an airfield tender and the original Bedford six-cylinder petrol engine was retained.

The specification of the Bedford Pyrene of the early 1950s is typical of the period when commercial airlines were getting into their stride after the enforced wartime curtailment of their activities. The performance and output seem meagre when compared with specifications current some twenty-five years later, but the size, speed and capacities of aircraft have also greatly increased in the same quarter of a century.

The Bedford QL chassis, which

was so well known by the end of the war, was not a surprising choice for the Bedford Pyrene; the Government had many that they no longer required and were ready to sell, and there were many in countries overseas which would probably never come back to

Below: Wartime Crossley 6 x 4 foam and CO_2 tender.

Bottom, left: German wartime semi-track converted for RAF airfield fire-fighting duties.

Bottom, right: Pyrene airfield crash tender mounted on a Bedford QL 4 x 4 military chassis.

Right: Basic hull, engine and controls of the Alvis 6 x 6 vehicle which formed the base for Pyrene and Foamite equipped aircraft crash tenders for the RAF.

Britain and from which a good supply of spare parts could be taken. The Pyrene Airfield Crash Tender also used another unit that had been proved during the war – the Coventry Climax petrol-engined centrifugal pump which established its pedigree during the incendiary air raids on Britain and was later modified and used in the Kieft, Lotus and Cooper racing cars that established Britain as a competitive force on the racing circuits of Europe.

SPECIFICATION

Engine: Bedford six-cylinder petrol, 3,519 cc, 72 bhp at 3,000 rpm

Transmission: Single dry plate clutch, four-speed gearbox, transfer box in front and rear axles

Brakes: Lockheed Hydraulic servo assisted

Tyres: 10.50 × 20

Dimensions: Length: 19 ft 10 in. (6.05 m)
Width: 7 ft 7 in. (2.31 m)
Height: 8 ft 6 in. (2.59 m)
Wheelbase: 11 ft 11 in. (3.63 m)
Track: 5 ft 8 in. (1.73 m)

The Coventry Climax pump unit had its own engine permanently coupled. The engine was a four-cylinder side-valve unit that developed 75 bhp at 3,000 rpm. The pump and its engine were mounted across the vehicle just behind the driver's compartment and immediately in front of the crew. At the rear of the crew's compartment were mounted six 50 lb (22.7 kg) CO_2 cylinders with

control cables running to the driver and discharge pipes connecting to the horns on the two hand-lines of 100 ft (30 m) of $\frac{1}{2}$ in. (12.5 mm) high-pressure hose carried on two hose-reels at the rear of the vehicle.

The main body of the vehicle contained a 500 gal (2,273 l) water-tank to the rear of the crew's cab and alongside it on the near side a 40 gal (181 l) foam-compound tank. Foam-discharge units were mounted at the extreme front of the vehicle on either side of the radiator grille in lockers which contained 80 ft (25 m) of 4 in. (10 cm) canvas hose and foam branches.

Alvis 6×6 Airfield Fire Crash Tender

During the 1950s the British Royal

Air Force took delivery of a number of highly mobile fire crash tenders which had a six-wheel format with all wheels driven and both front axles steering. The vehicle was adapted from the basic chassis components of the Army's FV 600 Alvis Salamander armoured car lower hull with the addition of a Rolls-Royce straight eight-cylinder petrol engine, light alloy road wheels, larger tyres, stiffer torsion bars, flow control steering and hydrovac braking. It was designed to negotiate all kinds of terrain at high speeds and to discharge 9,000 gal (40,900 l) of foam in two minutes from the roof monitor and two 60 ft (18.3 m)

side hoses.

The bodywork was completely enclosed, insulated and heated so that the vehicle was operational in all conditions. On vehicles that had bodywork by Foamite a longer monitor was used and the cab doors were hinged at the front. Appliances built by Pyrene had a short monitor and doors hinged at the rear.

Equipment included a Coventry Climax UFP 500 gal/min (2,273 l/min) pump driven via a full torque power take off from the engine at the back of the vehicle. Whenever the power take off was selected an air supercharger also came into operation to make foam.

The driver had controls for the roof monitor and side hoses, and a special integrating device which ensured that the air-water-foam mix was of proportions correct for the required output.

SPECIFICATION

Engine: Rolls-Royce B81 eight-cylinder petrol 6,500 cc 240 bhp

Transmission: Fluid coupling to Wilson five-speed pre-selector gearbox. Transfer box forward and reverse with power take off, articulating axles, dual epicyclic hub gearing

Brakes: Drums on all wheels, hydraulic footbrake, Hydrovac

servo all wheels, mechanical handbrake all wheels

Wheels: Light alloy WD divided disc

Tyres: 14.00 × 20

Suspension: Independent torsion bar, all wheels

Dimensions: Length: 18 ft (5.486 m)
Width: 8 ft 3 in. (2.515 m)
Height: 10 ft (3.048 m)
Wheelbase: 10 ft (3.048 m)
Track: 6 ft 8½ in. (2.045 m)

Chassis weight: 6 ton 3 cwt (6,249 kg)

Complete laden weight: 13 ton 10 cwt (13,717 kg)

Performance: Road, 45 mph (72 kph)
Cross country, 25 mph (40 kph)

Equipment: 500 gal/min (2,250 l/min) Coventry Climax pump
Roof monitor
Two 60 ft (18.3 m) side hoses
Two 100 ft (30.5 m) side hoses connected to 16 gal (73 l) chlorobromethane unit
Foam output 9,000 gal (40,900 l) in two minutes

Willeme SIDES VMA 75 and VREE 120 types

Before they ceased operations in 1970 the French chassis builders Willeme of Paris had produced both bonneted and cab-over versions of a 6×6 as the basis for numerous airfield crash tenders. The chassis and cab were made by Willeme and the fire-fighting equipment came from SIDES (Société Industrielle pour la Développement de la Sécurité) of Saint Nazaire.

The VMA 75 is the bonneted vehicle based on the Willeme W8DAE chassis powered by a Willeme straight eight-cylinder petrol engine of 330 hp. The SIDES equipment includes 1,430 gal (6,500 l) water capacity and 219 gal (1,000 l) of foam-compound. The centrifugal pump is powered by a separate Chevrolet six-cylinder petrol engine of 126 hp. There are two roof-mounted monitors each capable of producing 264 gal (1,200 l) of foam, and two side hoses of 110 gal/min (500 l/min) for operation up to 82 ft (25 m) from the appliance. Numerous items of equipment, including short extension ladders, are carried and

Left: Two of the powerful 8 x 8 Faun model LF/1410 airfield crash trucks employed at Munich airport with a wide-bodied jet aircraft in the background.

Above: Willeme/SIDES VMA 75 airfield fire tender for Paris airport.

ground-spray nozzles are located in the front fender.

The cab-over type VREE 120 has a similar chassis specification to the VMA but is somewhat shorter and lighter when unladen. SIDES equipment consists of a 2,640 gal (12,000 l) tank divided into two compartments – 2,420 gal (11,000 l) of water and 220 gal (1,000 l) of foam. Unlike the VMA 75, only one engine is used; the Willeme petrol engine being used for both propulsion and pumping. In addition to side hoses located just behind the cab there are two large-diameter hose-reels at the extreme rear end of the vehicle, each with 66 ft (20 m) of

2¾ in. (70 mm) hose. A further four outlets, two to each side, are located at the rear of the body.

SPECIFICATION

VMA 75

Road engine: Willeme eight-cylinder petrol 518-T8E 330 hp at 2,000 rpm

Transmission: six-speed gearbox, transfer box, drive to all axles. Power-assisted brakes and steering

Tyres: 1,600 × 25XR

Pump engine: Chevrolet six-cylinder petrol 126 hp at 3,800 rpm Total foam output possible 111½ ft/min (34 m/min)

Dimensions: Length: 32 ft 5¾ in. (9.9 m)
Width: 8 ft 4½ in. (2.550 m)
Height: 10 ft (3.050 m) top of cab 13 ft 1½ in. (4m) over monitor
Wheelbase: 13 ft 5⅝ in. + 4 ft 9⅛ in. (4.055 m + 1.450 m)

Weights: Chassis/cab: 13 tons (13.200 kg)
Bodywork & equipment: 3.44 tons (3,500 kg)
Liquids 7.77 tons (7,800 kg)
Total all up weight 24.1 tons (24,500 kg)

Performance: Standing start to ⅝ mile (1 km), 68 seconds
60 seconds from standing start to 46.6 mph (75 kph)
Top speed 59 mph (95 kph)

VREE 120

Engine: Willeme eight-cylinder petrol 518-T8E 330 hp to 2,000 rpm

Transmission: six-speed gearbox, transfer box, drive to all axles, power-assisted steering and brakes

Tyres: 16.00 × 25 XR

Top: The lighter VREE 120 model of the Willeme 6 x 6 airfield crash tender for Paris.

Centre: A 1959 Volvo 6 x 6 aircraft crash tender for the Swedish air force.

Bottom: Kaelble/Kronenburg 4 x 4 airfield crash truck pictured during a training session at Stuttgart airport.

Dimensions: Length: 30 ft 6 in. (9.300 m)
Width: 8 ft 2½ in. (2.500 m)
Height: 9 ft 10 in. (3 m) to cab roof
10 ft 8 in. (3.250 m) over searchlight
Wheelbase: 13 ft 7½ in. +5ft 5 in. (4.150 m +1.650 m)

Weights: Chassis/cab: 11.71 tons (11,900 kg)
Body and equipment: 3.93 tons (4,000 kg)
Liquids: 11.9 tons (12,100 kg)
Total all up weight: 27.5 tons (28,000 kg)

Performance: Standing start to ⅝ mile (1 km), 70 seconds

60 seconds from standing start to 43½ mph (70 kph)
Top speed: 56 mph (90 kph)

Kaelble KV600F (FLF 66) Kronenburg

Kaelble have a history going back to 1925 and have been involved in making steam traction engines, crawler agricultural tractors, and petrol- and oil-engined heavy trucks for use on and off highways. Besides heavy chassis for use in fire-fighting, current production includes heavy-duty road tractors, dump-trucks, crane carriers and special vehicles for use in foundries. Their entry into the sphere of fire-fighting was recent, and they

incline to specialising in substantial chassis for turntable-ladders and airfield crash tenders such as the one under review.

The Kaelble KV600F is based on a straightforward 4×4 chassis with two separate engines for powering the vehicle and pump. The channel-section chassis frame is flat and level on the top. It is 4 ft 9½ in. (1.460 m) wide from the rear end to a point just behind the front axle: here, where the driving engine and forward-mounted cab are located, it narrows sharply to

Below: Twin-engined 4 x 4 Kaelble/ Kronenburg FLF66 airfield crash tender.

a mere 2 ft 7½ in. (80 cm). The vehicle has left-hand steering and to the right of the driver, where a short ladder gives access to the roof-mounted monitor, there is room for two of the crew.

Immediately behind the driver there is the main vehicle engine, a 6,600 hp Daimler-Benz unit coupled directly to an Allison six-speed gearbox and torque converter. A short propeller shaft takes the drive to the Kaelble transfer box where power is apportioned to front and rear axles.

At the extreme rear of the chassis the pump engine is mounted transversely and bolted to it there is a two-stage centrifugal pump with its associated piping. The centre of the vehicle is taken up by a 1,760 gal (8,000 l) water-

tank and a foam-tank of 220 gal (1,000 l) capacity. Both tanks, constructed of steel, are spring-mounted to absorb road shocks and twisting of the chassis.

Dispensing equipment consists of the roof-mounted monitor of 440 gal/min (2,000 l/min) capacity, two removable side hose-reels each of 44 gal/min (200 l/min) capacity, three forward-facing jets just below the front fender with a total output of 66 gal/min (300 l/min), and two underfloor jets of 13 gal/min (60 l/min) to protect the tyres and underside of the vehicle from blazing fuel or debris.

SPECIFICATION

Engine: Daimler-Benz 6V331 TC, six-cylinder 22–44 litre, 600 hp at 2,200 rpm

Top, left: Lightwieght airfield fire truck by Fire-X on an International 4 x 4 chassis.

Top, right: Heavy duty aircraft fire and rescue truck by Fire-X mounted on a 6 x 6 chassis with a Cummins 12-cylinder engine at the rear.

Above, left: Saval-Kronenburg 4 x 4 MAC D4 model for service at a Turkish airport.

Above, right: Skuteng airfield tender on a Tatra 6 x 6 chassis.

Right: Oshkosh M1500 6 x 6 airfield crash and rescue truck.

Transmission: Allison power shift with torque converter Kaelble transfer box

Tyres: 23.5-25K type Michelin

Brakes: Air pressure, dual circuit: spring emergency, air actuated

Pump Engine: Daimler-Benz six-cylinder OM-346 2.4 gal

(10.810 l) 180 hp at 2,200 rpm

Dimensions: Length 31 ft 10 in.
(9.710 m) chassis/cab
Width: 10 ft 2 in. (3.100 m)
chassis/cab
Height: 10 ft (3.050 m)
chassis/cab

Performance: Standing start to
50 mph (80 kph) in 45 seconds
Top speed 62 mph (100 kph)

Oshkosh Truck Corporation of Oshkosh, Wisconsin

Oshkosh are among the world's
large manufacturers of specialised
airfield crash and rescue vehicles
and build four-, six- and eight-
wheel types featuring single- and
twin-engined layouts.

The M1000 is one of their smaller
units but it has an impressive
specification which includes a

Caterpillar 3406 engine rated at
335 hp at 2,100 rpm, an integral
four-speed gearbox and
transmission transfer box with
driver control of positive all-wheel
drive. The engine mounted at the
rear leaves the cab free for the four-
man crew, although the vehicle
can be handled by the driver alone
if necessary. Fire-fighting
equipment includes a 1,000 gal
(4,546 l) water-tank and 135 gal
(614 l) foam-tank and a single-
stage centrifugal pump driven by
an independent 210 hp V8
engine. Discharge is via a roof
monitor, two side hoses of 100 ft
(30 m) on hose-reels, two forward-
mounted ground-sweep nozzles
and a pair of undertruck nozzles to
protect the tyres.

The vehicle is designed as three
independent units – cab, main

body and engine – that can move
separately as the chassis frame
flexes while moving over
undulating ground. Diagonally-
opposite wheels can lift 14 in.
(35.6 cm) without losing traction,
and the vehicle can be driven up a
sixty per cent gradient and operate
on a twenty per cent side slope. Its
speeds of 50 mph (80 kph) in
thirty-five seconds from start and
at 60 mph (96 kph) for cruising
enable it to respond quickly to
calls.

The M1500 is a six-wheel
configuration which features all-
wheel drive and three-section
layout (cab, main body, engine) but
employs only one large engine for
both traction and pumping. Its
capacity is 1,500 gal (6,819 l) of
water and 180 gal (545 l) of foam-
concentrate feeding a roof

monitor of 400–800 gal/min
(1,818–3,636 l/min) dual rate, a
300 gal (1,363 l) bumper monitor
with ground-sweep to within
20 ft (6.1 m) of the front of the
vehicle, and a side hand-line of
100 gal (454 l) foam and 50 gal
(227 l) water capacity for close
work. The six-cylinder 15 litre
(893 cu in.) engine produces
425 hp at 2,100 rpm and drives
through a power divider when
pumping is required whilst the
vehicle is in motion.

A notable feature of the M1500
is its stowage for 500 ft (152 m) of
2½ in. (6.35 cm) hose and 300 ft
(91 m) of 1½ in. (3.8 cm) hose
together with hydrant connections
and suction inlets so that it can
double as a class A 1,000 gal/min
(4,546 l/min) pumper for airport
protection duties in addition to its
role of airfield crash and rescue
vehicle.

The Oshkosh range of four eight-
wheel vehicles consists of three for
civilian use – M3000, M4000 and
M6000 – and the P15 for military
use. They are all based on a similar
layout which embodies four axles
and dual engines and varies only in
detail of equipment and tank
capacities.

SPECIFICATION

**US Air Force P15 crash/rescue
vehicle**
Engines: Two (front and rear)
Detroit Diesel 8V92T 12 litre
(736 cu in.) 430 hp at 2,100 rpm

Transmission: Torque converter
to Oshkosh seven-speed powershift
gearbox, planetary drive to wheels,
all differentials lockable

Tyres: 26.5 × 25

Dimensions: Length: 45 ft 2 in.
(13.76 m) excluding monitors
Width: 9 ft 11 in. (3.04 m)
Height: 13 ft 9 in. (4.19 m) over
monitors
Wheelbase: 25 ft 4 in. (7.72 m)
bogie centres
Track: 7 ft 9 in. (2.37 m)

Weights: Unladen, 30.67 tons
(31.161 kg)
Operational, 55.41 tons
(56,306 kg)

Performance: 0 to 50 mph
(80 kph) in 70 seconds
Top speed 50 mph (80 kph)
Ascend and descend 60% gradient
Side slope stability in excess
of 50%
Will climb a wall 18 in. (45.7 cm)
high

Equipment: Two single-stage
centrifugal pumps of 200 gal/min
(757 l/min) capacity for foam
discharge
Two single-stage centrifugal pumps
of 1,250 gal/min (4,732 l/min)
capacity for water discharge
6,000 gal (22,712 l) water-tank
515 gal (1,950 l) foam-tank
Hand-line on right side with
150 ft (46 m) hose stowed on reel
100 gal/min (379 l/min) foam or
50 gal/min (189 l/min) water

Top: A mid-1950s Czechoslovak
Tatra airfield crash tender in service
at Torslanda airport, Gothenburg.

Above: The mighty Oshkosh 8 x 8
military pattern P15 airfield fire and
crash truck.

Front- and rear-facing roof
monitors rated at 1,200 gal/min
(4,542 l/min) for foam and
600 gal/min (2,271 l/min) for
water

Other astonishing data show
that in fire-fighting trim the P15
weighs more than an US Army
main battle tank, that its tyres
contain enough rubber to make
232 standard automobile tyres, and
that when the main water-tank
is discharged for foam-making it

can cover a football field to a depth of 2 in. (5 cm) or a baseball court to a depth of 2 ft (60 cm) in two and a half minutes.

The Jumbo age of fire-fighting was established by the appearance in the late 1960s of Faun's pair of 8×8 foam-trucks and an 8×8 dry-powder tender for Frankfurt airport. They were not the first eight-wheeled fire apparatus – a considerable number of FWD 8×8s were built in the middle 1960s – but the Fauns, with bodywork and equipment by

other long-distance aircraft and the potential threat to a similarly larger number of passengers. They decided that their precautions should not take the form of an increased number of standard crash tenders, which would probably only get in each other's way when they were needed to be at their utmost efficiency. Instead, they were convinced that their equipment had to match the size of the problem and its cause if they were to stand any chance of dealing successfully with an emergency of fearful magnitude.

and is designed to prevent re-ignition. Priority has, of course, been given to extinguishing fire, for it is only after fire has been put out that rescue can be attempted.

Another important task of airfield emergency services is to prepare the runway for an aircraft that might have to make a forced landing. The most important need is to prevent a skidding aircraft from making sparks that could ignite spilled fuel. This is done by laying a thick carpet of foam from a three-axle vehicle equipped with numerous nozzles arranged in a

Metz and Total, impressively confirmed the trend.

The need for enormous fire appliances at airfields followed the design of the Boeing 747 Jumbo Jet. The aircraft's huge fuselage (longer than the height of a twenty-storey building, with a cockpit as high from the ground as the roof of a three-storey house), its great carrying capacity (up to 490 passengers), and its frightening load of 39,700 gal (180,000 l) of fuel made some measure to counter disaster imperative.

The airport authorities at Frankfurt studied the problems of an emergency in which a Boeing 747 could be involved. They considered the danger from bulk fuel which amounted to at least double the quantity carried by

The result of close collaboration between manufacturers of fire-fighting equipment and the authorities at Frankfurt airport was a new generation of fire and rescue trucks that conformed to the highest standards of the day and gave enhanced speed, capacity, rate of discharge and area of coverage.

In operation, the three giant Faun vehicles work together as a team. The first strike is by the dry-powder tender which can hurl up to 224 lb (100 kg) of extinguishing powder as far as 200 ft (60 m). The function of this powder is to stop oxygen getting to the fire. This is followed by a layer of foam which is discharged by the foam-tenders at a combined rate of 17,600 gallons (80,000 l) a minute

Above: The Oshkosh shows its paces close to the press.

wide arc and of 8,800 gal (40,000 l) capacity, made up of 8,250 gal (37,500 l) of water and 550 gal (2,500 l) of foam-making agent.

Ward La France Statesman Crash and Rescue Vehicle
Current production includes a range of 4×4 airfield crash and rescue vehicles which fall into two main categories: Statesman Class III as a medium type of crash truck, and Class II as a heavy-duty model. Both employ two rear-mounted engines and carry 3,000 gal (13,638 l) tanks.

SPECIFICATION

Statesman Class III

Engines: Two Detroit Diesel 8V71 V8 350 hp at 2,300 rpm, 9,289 cc (568 cu in.), one for powering vehicle, one for pump

Transmission: Automatic four-speed gearbox and torque converter to centre transfer box thence to both axles

Tyres: 14.5 × 25

Dimensions: Length: 28 ft 11 in. (8.81 m)
Width: 8 ft 4 in. (2.54 m)
Height: 12 ft (3.65 m)
Wheelbase: 16 ft 8 in. (5.08 m)
Track: 6 ft 10 in. (2.08 m)

Equipment: Hale FRQ single-stage centrifugal pump centrally mounted, 1,400 gal/min (6,358 l/min), 3,000 gal (13,638 l) water-tank, 300 gal (1,364 l) foam-tank
Roof monitor 400 or 800 gal/min (1,818/3,636 l/min)
Ground-sweep nozzle just below front bumper
Two underbody nozzles

Two side hose-reels

SPECIFICATION

Statesman Class IV

Engines: Two Detroit Diesel 6V53 432 hp at 2,800 rpm, both driving through flywheel power take off to centre transfer box and thence to both axles

Transmission: Power shift with torque converter

Tyres: 23.5 × 25

Dimensions: Length: 31 ft 4 in. (9.55 m)
Width: 10 ft (3.04 m)
Height: 12 ft 10 in. (3.91 m)
Wheelbase: 17 ft 6 in. (5.33 m)
Track: 8 ft (2.43 m)

Equipment: Two Hale 50FR-U3600 single-stage centrifugal pumps each of 750 gal/min (3,342 l/min) capacity driven by a separate engine. Either one or both pumps can be used at any time: 3,000 gal (13,638 l) water-tank, 500 gal (2,270 l) foam capacity being in two 250 gal (932 l) neoprene bladders installed in the bottom of the water-tank
Roof monitor of 500 or 1,000 gal/min (2,273/4,546 l/min) dual capacity
One ground-sweep nozzle, just below front bumper

Left, above: Ward La France Statesman with ultra-vision cab and two rear engines.

Left, below: Saval-Kronenburg 8 x 8 airfield crash truck.

Right: SIDES-equipped Berliet airfield crash truck.

Below: First of the Scammell 6 x 6 rear-engined chassis for airfield fire trucks use being put through its paces over a military test track.

Two underbody nozzles
Two swing-out side hose-reels

Vickers AWD/Carmichael Jetranger 3000

This is a high-performance 6×6 rear-engined chassis specially produced by Vickers All Wheel Drive, who applied their experience of special chassis for cross-country and crane carrier work to its production. During a *Commercial Motor* test of the loaded chassis at the Military Vehicles and Engineering Establishment in 1971 the vehicle put up a creditable performance under far more severe conditions than would be encountered in service. At an all up weight of 33½ tons (34,036 kg) acceleration up to 60 mph (96 kph) was achieved in forty-two seconds, and on the cross-country course the vehicle was stopped and restarted on a one in three gradient. When completed with bodywork and equipment by Carmichael several vehicles were exported to South Africa.

SPECIFICATION

Engine: Cummins VTA 1700-170 V12 700 hp at 2,100 rpm located at rear

Transmission: Twin Disc torque converter and six-speed semi-automatic gearbox to Scammell rear bogie and AEC front axle

Tyres: Michelin X5 14×20 front; 24×20.5 rear

Dimensions: Length: 35 ft 4 in. (10.77 m)
Width: 9 ft (2.74 m)
Height: 12 ft (3.65 m)
Wheelbase: 17 ft (5.18 m)

Weights: Chassis only: 13 ton

2 cwt (13,309 kg)
Gross: 33½ tons (34,036 kg)

Equipment: Water-tank:
2,452 gal (12,146 l)
Foam-tank: 415 gal (1,886 l)
Roof monitor, ground-sweep
sprays, underbody nozzles and
two side-lines or hose-reels
Single pump is driven by a power
take off behind the torque
converter and can be engaged and
disengaged while the vehicle is
travelling
Monitor projects up to 250 ft
(76.2 m) at a rate of 10,000

gal/min (45,460 l/min)

Performance: 0 to 60 mph
(96 kph) in 42 seconds
Top speed 70 mph (112 kph)

The Thornycroft Nubian Major
has had a long career in the world
of fire-fighting since it was
introduced in the early 1950s after
the 4 × 4 Nubian, suitable as it was
as the basis for an airfield fire
tender, was found to lack the
body space required to cope with
the size of aircraft being produced.
In its original form, the

In 1977 the Nubian Major was
succeeded by the Scammell
Nubian. This model was available
in 4 × 4 and 6 × 6 forms and, as
each configuration had two
different power models, it acquired
four names – Nubian 2, Super
Nubian, Nubian Major 2 and
Super Major.

The Cummins engine has again
been chosen to power the new
chassis, but this time from the rear,
and the same basic engine is
available in three different versions
to produce outputs of approximately
300, 400 and 500 brake

**Above: Carmichael 'Jetranger' for
Rhoose airport at a training aircraft
'fire'.**

**Left: Thornycroft/HCB 6 x 6
destined for service in Malaysia.**

Thornycroft six-cylinder oil
engine and the Rolls-Royce eight-
cylinder petrol engine were
offered as alternatives, but during
its life the chassis has also been
available with the later B81 Rolls-
Royce petrol engine, a Cummins
V8 diesel engine, or the AEC
four-cylinder AV 410 diesel. It has
been a popular chassis among
builders of fire equipment in
Britain and elsewhere: numbered
among its users have been Pyrene,
Airfoam, Sun, Merryweather,
Dennis, Gloster Saro, Carmichael,
HCB Angus, Miles and SIDES, and
it has seen service in many parts
of the world during the last
twenty-five years.

horsepower to suit varying
conditions. A completely new
design of pressed-steel cab with a
low overall height, which can be
extended at the back if necessary,
is offered as part of the design.
The production cab seats three,
and steering may be at the left or
right, or in the centre, as chosen.

In the antipodes, Presha
Engineering Pty Ltd of Victoria
generally supply airfield crash
tenders to the Australian continent
and to south-east Asia. A number
of different models are made in
Australia and they include a light
rescue tender built on a Jeep 4 × 4
chassis, a medium fire tender on a
Bedford R 4 × 4 or similar
middleweight chassis, and a large
6 × 6 CT 2000 airfield fire tender
based on the Australian RFW
chassis. Presha have supplied
vehicles to civil and military
airfields in Australia, Malaya,
Indonesia, New Guinea, Nepal
and the Philippines.

BUILDING A FIRE ENGINE

The best way to see how a fire appliance is built is to look at and follow the processes that take place in the manufacturer's organisation. The starting point is usually an enquiry from a potential customer. The enquiry might come because the manufacturer's own sales staff has solicited interest. Or perhaps one of the builder's appliances has been noticed at an exhibition, or in an advertisement. A likely cause is the builder's reputation among fire-fighting people and their automatic consideration of his skill and products when they need new equipment.

A manufacturer's own organisation will play a large part in securing enquiries and in converting or failing to convert enquiries into orders. An efficient sales staff in such a specialised field should have some knowledge of possible requirements among fire authorities around the world and be able to give quick comparisons between their own products, services and prices and those of their competitors. The builder's designers can reassure hesitant clients, and the promise of reliability over workmanship, delivery and price will be just as important.

The enquiry itself can take one of a number of different forms. It might be explicit, with an exact and complete specification that has been drawn up by the client's own staff. It might come from a small town or factory and vaguely ask about a 'fire engine' to replace an ageing appliance. Between these two extremes come all manner of enquiries ranging from those who know exactly what they would like – though often with little idea about how to cram all the equipment on one vehicle – to those who just know that they want a vehicle to be ready at short notice to handle their emergencies. And emergencies become increasingly varied : at one time a fire engine was to put out fires but today it is more of an

Left: Mercedes-Benz with Metz 30-metre turntable-ladder.

Above, right: A Dennis turntable-ladder at the Annual Conference of British Fire Officers at Brighton, 1977. The latest vehicles and equipment in fire fighting are shown off at such exhibitions.

Right: A bare chassis and cab await the fitting of a Simon Snorkel at the Dudley factory.

emergency vehicle ready to deal with all kinds of problems, from small boys with heads stuck in railings up to explosions at chemical factories which produce poison gases.

Whatever the enquiry, the sales staff, the design department and the planners of production will work together to form a quotation. Part of the quotation will, of course, concern price, which is likely to be affected by the probable need to obtain certain parts or equipment from outside specialist suppliers over whose prices there will be little internal control. The quotation will, therefore, include a date after which the price is not guaranteed to be firm.

When an order is secured a detailed specification will be drawn up which lists everything about the vehicle; general description, engine type, pump type, locker arrangement, crew compartment, ladder positions, lights, hose stowage, piping layout, water/foam-tank capacities and position, electrical fittings, loose equipment, painting and lettering, and shipping or delivery arrangements. A works schedule is also prepared which is similar to the specification but goes into greater detail including drawings and illustrations to be used in the actual construction of the vehicle. The production planning department will prepare a list of parts, equipment and materials required and advise the stores who will order anything which is not

a stock item, taking due note of the date production is scheduled to begin. While some items may be obtained 'off the shelf' others may have far off delivery dates and it may be necessary to obtain alternatives if a long delay is to be avoided.

Most builders of medium-sized fire appliances use proprietary chassis as a basis for their vehicles and alter them to meet requirements. Thus, according to the type of vehicle required, there

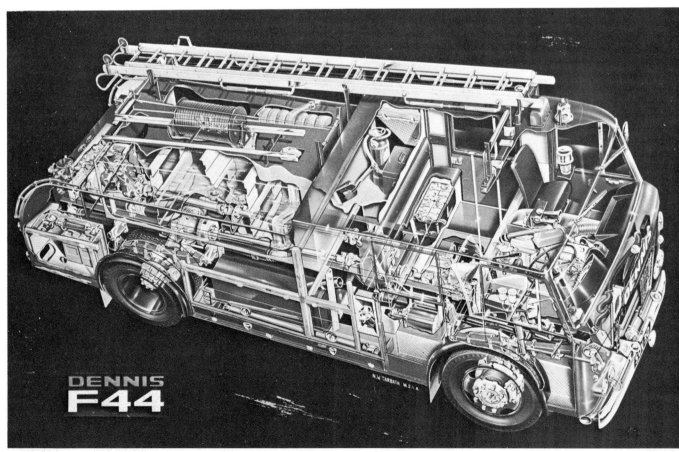

DENNIS F44

Facing page, above: A scene inside a bodyshop as work proceeds on cabs and bodies of AEC chassis.

Facing page, below: Artist's drawing showing a ghosted view of a Dennis F44 appliance.

Below, left: A Dennis chassis with only the cab-framing and water-tank in position.

Below, right: A normal Land-Rover chassis being converted to forward control in the Carmichael factory.

Bottom: A Range Rover before the third axle and bodywork are fitted in the Carmichael factory.

may be minimal alterations to a standard production van or truck or there may be extensive alterations with some original parts being cut off and discarded. This is costly and is avoided whenever possible, but it is often expedient to take a standard truck chassis with cab and alter it as desired by the customer rather than have a complete chassis purpose built.

Depending on the design, we may start with a plain chassis which has only the controls and

a rough wooden seat. Such would be the case if a completely new large crew cab was to be built on the chassis and in which event the original truck cab would be of no use. An alternative is termed 'chassis/scuttle' and consists of a chassis complete with proper upholstered driver's seat, controls and front panel of the cab complete with windscreen. This would be the basis of a vehicle which did not require a completely integrated cab and crew compartment; although such

features could be provided by body-builders through a fairing or joining panel between the cab front and the body proper.

Where alteration is to be kept to a minimum the complete cab can be utilised and the fire appliance bodywork attached to the rear – although with a crew compartment just to the rear of the original cab it is better to remove the back of the cab so that communication between the two sections is possible.

Whatever the configuration, the chassis will first go to the engineering shops where all the alterations, removals and additions will be effected. This is where the basic truck chassis is converted to carry specialist equipment. The work to be done may be slight, such as providing a power take off ready to drive the pump and fit out-riggers to the chassis frame in order to attach the body of the appliance. On the other hand, the work to be done could be considerable. For example: if only a 4×4 chassis is available (a chassis with all four wheels driving) and a 6×6 is required (one with all six wheels being driven), then the chassis frame would have to be lengthened, another driving axle fitted and drive shafts and suspension added.

On vehicles where the engine is used to power the fire pump it is usual to fit a heat exchanger at this stage so that in service the

Left: A view inside the Leyland fire engine shop in 1937 with work progressing on turntable-ladders and other appliances.

Below: A general view of a fire engine works showing vehicles in the course of construction.

engine does not get overheated. The action of this heat exchanger is to provide the engine with a continual flow of water for cooling purposes when pumping, as opposed to the more usual closed-circuit system when the engine is used merely for propulsion.

While work is proceeding on the chassis the bodywork is being prepared in the bodyshop, but before the body can be fitted to the chassis it is necessary for the tank or tanks to be secured to the chassis. The construction, positioning and fitting of the water/foam-tanks is of the utmost importance because they form the largest and heaviest single item save that of mechanical ladders or hydraulic platforms. The early use of copper or steel for tanks has now given way to glass-fibre construction, which can be moulded to a greater variety of sizes and shapes and is lighter in weight. But these tanks do not possess the inherent strength of metal and are liable to crumple if the vehicle should roll over.

On tanker-type vehicles with large-capacity tanks it is important that the tanks be mounted in such a way as to allow the chassis to 'flex' under operating conditions. This means that in practice the medium-size tanks are rigidly attached to the chassis frame at the rear while the front end of the tank is attached to a flexible mounting bolted to a chassis

Right: Water tests being carried out on an incomplete Thornycroft airfield tender in the Dennis works.

Below: Inside the Oshkosh works an M1500 airfield crash truck begins to take shape.

cross-member. With the very large tanks used on six- and eight-wheel airfield crash tenders the tanks would be mounted on six or eight flexible rubber mountings.

After fitting the main pump and the appropriate piping the tank is filled, the pump is tested and the system checked for water leaks. When the tests of the pumps have been satisfactorily completed the vehicle goes for painting of all the work so far completed. The next task is to mount the body on the chassis/tank/pump as it is so far assembled, care being taken to paint the underside of the body and the interior of the tank

Right: Rear end of a Magirus chassis showing the pump fitted and the drive shaft positioned below grp water-tank.

Below: General view of the Simon Snorkel fitting shop at Dudley.

compartment before lowering the body onto the chassis.

It is probable that the body of the modern fire appliance will be of composite construction; that is to say a mixture of metal, wood and glass-fibre. In a typical design we find that the front part of the vehicle, including the driver's cab and crew compartment,

corrugation or by adding valleys or channels to accommodate items of equipment. This is done when forming the roof section of an airfield crash tender which has an aperture for operation of the roof-mounted foam-monitor. Here it is desirable to form supporting ribs in the roof for a frame to edge the aperture and

road performance and it must therefore be rigid, light and powerful; in other words, have a good power-to-weight ratio. With the varied nature of emergencies increasing every day, the list of diverse equipment to be carried is constantly lengthening. The bare body weight has to be kept down without reducing

Above, left: Bodywork proceeding on a SD/Carmichael airfield crash tender.

Above: Nearing completion: a signwriter puts the finishing touches to a Carmichael appliance in the paintshop.

is largely of glass-reinforced plastics, which consists of finely stranded glass-fibre matting positioned in a mould of the required shape and impregnated with a special non-inflammable resin in liquid form. The mixture is rolled out thoroughly by hand-roller to ensure adequate bonding of the resin with the stranded glass-fibre and then left to 'cure' for about twenty-four hours. When it is hard the section is removed from the mould and prepared for fitting to the vehicle. Although the resulting panel or section is quite strong in itself it is often necessary to strengthen the part by the addition of bars, angles, plates and sheets, these being of wood, steel, aluminium, or even solid plastic-foam when lightness is important.

These strengthening parts are placed in the mould during the forming of the component and so become an integral part of the whole. In similar fashion, bolts or other fastening devices can be absorbed into a monolithic section in preparation for attachment to another, and a roof moulding can be increased in strength by

the roof itself is then strong enough to take the agitation of the monitor as the foam is pumped through it. The weight of the monitor is taken by the vertical foam-delivery pipe. The cab roof has a perforated aluminium plate moulded in with the roof section to act as a 'ground' for the vehicle's communicating system.

The main bodywork section that covers the remainder of the body will probably be made of light alloy. Parts that are to be painted will be etched to form a 'key' for the paint while those to be left unpainted usually have a shallow surface pattern to obscure little marks sustained in service. Parts and areas subject to heavy traffic will be of harder-wearing tread pattern. Locker lids and doors might be of aluminium or glass-reinforced plastic, while rolling shutters are normally of alloy. Locker divisions, crew compartment linings, and other sundry small parts will be of plywood, unless they are likely to be subjected to much wear, in which case they will be made of aluminium.

A fire appliance must have good

strength and rigidity, for, should the vehicle become involved in an accident the safety of the crew is paramount. Where a glass-reinforced plastic body might crumple at the point of impact a blow sustained on a metal body can be transmitted right down the vehicle. But bodywork that is light and flimsy could, in an accident, flatten down to the chassis frame with disastrous results.

As we have seen, some construction of the body would have taken place whilst work was proceeding on the chassis by the engineering department. The extent of this work on the body would have been considerable but not complete. The main shape of the body would have been built up in glass-reinforced plastic or alloy, and the work would have included shutters, locker lids, main equipment positioning, attaching fittings for later attachment of loose equipment, ladder fittings and gantries, some electrical fittings and wiring, ladders or steps to the roof, handrails, walkways and roof fittings; and the interior would have been painted.

After attaching the body to the chassis, the joint to the original cab or cowl would be made good by fitting glass-reinforced plastic fairing or some other appropriate material. If the vehicle had a tilt cab it would be necessary to place a rubber weather-proof seal between cab and body sections and to check that nothing fouled the tilting of the cab.

Seats for the crew are now added by the trimming shop; the remaining small fittings are attached and the electrical wiring completed. With the vehicle in this state a second test is made to the pump and the piping, joints, and hoses, and nozzles are checked for leaks and rectified as necessary. The vehicle then goes to the paintshop for finishing coats according to the specification and then on to the finishing-shop for the attachment of labels, instruction plates, transfers and lettering. Export vehicles are specially prepared to withstand the rigours of their journeys with some of the smaller items of equipment being packed and protected to guard against possible damage or corrosion. Domestic vehicles have the remainder of their equipment attached prior to receiving a final inspection vis-à-vis the specification.

The completed vehicle is given a final test of its pumps and a full road test to check performance. A tilt test to check the degree of sway that is possible without the vehicle rolling over will add to the appliance's bill of health. In these final tests the total weight of the crew will be simulated by ballast.

The completed appliance is now offered for delivery and is usually subjected to an acceptance check by the customer.

Left: A Dennis/Simon Snorkel undergoes final checks and testing before being presented to the customer for approval and acceptance.

Below: A scene outside the Oshkosh works as a completed truck is drawn alongside a bare chassis/cab.

THE FIRE-FIGHTERS

There must be few people who do not feel a thrill of excitement when they see fire-fighters going to a fire, or actually fighting it. Of course, we all carry into our later years memories of our childhood days when everything seemed twice as large as life and powerful fire engine drivers and confident fire-fighters handled their jobs with panache, speed and pride.

Period photographs of fire-fighters give the impression of tough, resolute and dedicated men ready and able to tackle the hazards they are called upon to face. They stand very still while the photographer carefully removes his lens-cap, pauses and replaces it with equal care. Only the horses twitch their ears or move their heads slightly, puzzled why they should stand so still when normally they are being urged forward at all possible speed. The steamer, hose-cart or ladder-truck in the background is in matchless condition after hours of devoted cleaning and polishing.

The years roll by and we find another photograph of fire-fighters – but things are different. Gone are the steam pumps, the brass helmets, the horses, the shining appliance. The men look grim, dirty, tired to gauntness. It is a time of war, and in the grained photograph everything is either dark or grey. The apparatus is grey, the men look grey and the sky is dark with smoke. But, for all this, the men are the same as their predecessors – tired but tough, weary but willing, grimy but full of grit and determination.

Times change again and we come to the present day and compare the turnout as before. Suddenly everything is colourful

Below: A Rosenbauer-equipped Volkswagen seen in action with a German crew.

and bright, the crisp coloured photograph captures everything as large and sharp as life, bright apparatus, leggings, helmets, equipment – all in a wide variety of colours. Important colours, too – not just for show as in the old days. Easily recognised colours, reds, lime green, reflective orange, bright blue, crisp white, bold yellow, each has an important meaning to the men who use the apparatus. Amidst all the colour there remains the every-day attitude of the fire-fighters – just as always, calm, courageous and confident.

It is difficult to be exact about who had the first fire brigade or company of firemen as such. Of course, as one would expect, the Romans organised theirs along military lines and, of course, France still does. Following the decline of the Roman empire the organisation of public services such as fire-fighting seems to have fallen into neglect, or, at least, there is little to suggest otherwise.

From such records as there are, it would appear that continental Europe reawakened to fire prevention and fire-fighting about the fourteenth century for there is mention of organised fire precautions in 1371. These precautions took the form of ordering that each house should have a barrel of water placed by the door and that the firing of guns and the burning of straw in the streets was forbidden. In 1670 in France all masons, carpenters and tilers were ordered to give their names to the police, and they and their employees had to report for duty upon the fire-alarm being sounded. As early as 1521 regulations for combating fire were issued in Saxony, while there had been earlier laws in many towns requiring that a look-out be posted at the top of a high building and that he should ring a bell and point a flag in the direction of the fire.

No doubt there were even earlier regulations and arrangements in large continental towns, for in London there are records showing that in 1189 the ward-motes of the City arranged that occupants of great houses within the ward have a ladder or two ready and prepared to succour their neighbours in case misadventure should occur from 'fire', and that during summertime 'and especially between the feast of Pentecost and the feast of St Bartholomew, before their doors a barrel full of water for quenching such fires, if it be not a house which has a fountain of its own'. In addition it was decided that 'ten reputable men of the ward, with ten aldermen, provide a strong crook of iron with a wooden handle, together with

Below: Firemen with Mack Aerialscope CF pumper at work as seen from the air.

two chains and two strong cords, and that the beadle have a good horn and loudly sounding'.

By 1268 a night watch had been arranged for the City of London and in 1285 Edward I passed an Act ordering that similar watches be provided in every·large town and city in the realm. In 1472 the town of Exeter decided to appoint a bellman and London took up the idea in 1556, instructing him to walk the streets crying 'Take care of your fire and candle, be charitable to the poor, and pray for the dead' ! Exeter also decided that leather buckets, iron crooks and ladders be placed in readiness for fire in 1558, and other towns followed suit soon after. Naturally, communications were slow but with the news of bad fires being talked about across the country more towns and parishes decided that such items as buckets, ladders, axes and hooks should be obtained and stored in prominent places in their areas. Much of the early records is about the items of equipment, and how the handling of these items was left to such people as mayors, aldermen, masons and the general public. No one seemed to think it necessary to organise bodies of trained people who could be relied on to carry out fire-fighting in an efficient manner.

Continental Europe was ahead of Britain in the formation of fire-fighters, for in Germany, Holland, France and Switzerland volunteer brigades were organised during the seventeeth century. In Britain it took the disastrous Great Fire of London of 1666 to make an impression on authority, and the following year there was much activity connected with the provision of more equipment, stringent building regulations and the provision of a good supply of water.

Naturally, as the old City of London had suffered from the great conflagration it was principally to that city that the majority of the legislation was directed. Anyway, there was nothing really wrong in the premise that 'if we do it in London today the provincial town can do it tomorrow'. So the new City was divided into four districts and 'each thereof was to be provided with eight hundred leather buckets, fifty ladders of different sizes, from twelve to forty-two feet in length (3.6 m to 12.8 m), two brazen hand-squirts to each parish, four and twenty pickaxe sledges, and forty shod shovels'. The requirements went on 'that each of the twelve companies provide themselves with an engine, thirty buckets, three ladders, six pickaxe sledges, and two hand-squirts, to be ready on all occasions'. Other provisions were given for 'inferior companies' (smaller) who were to get a supply of small engines and buckets

"A Turn Out" Islington Fire Station.

Above, left: Men and equipment of the Broken Hill Fire Brigade, probably around 1900. The left-hand machine in this picture by the Australian Historical Society of Fire Engines is a locally built Bawn manual.

Left: A turn out at Islington Fire Station, London, at the beginning of the century.

Right: A Hook and Ladder Company, with a vehicle steered at both ends, turns out for a fire in New York City; from 'Harper's Weekly', 7 March 1891.

allotted to them. Pumps were to be put in all the wells and fire-plugs in several of the main water-pipes of the New River and Thames waterworks.

Still there were no provisions for fire brigades as such, although this was the time of the van der Heijdens who were doing great business with their new fire engines in Holland where fire-fighting was taken seriously and there was already a municipal fire brigade equipped with sixty engines in Amsterdam.

Britain found an answer to the problem of trained manpower for fire-fighting in the formation of insurance brigades soon after the fire of 1666. Nicholas Barbon and his associates opened the first regular office for assuring against loss by fire, and from their room 'at the back side of the Royal Exchange' they began

operations in 1681. Their Fire Office did not remain the only enterprise of its kind for long. Others soon saw that there was good business to be done so long as the various properties and goods insured could be given some form of protection in order to lower the risk of loss. Before long, there were established private bodies of organised fire-fighters complete with equipment ready to protect the insurance companies' policy holders. The Hand-in-Hand had a fire engine and band of fire-fighters in 1699. Other early companies were the Sun (1710), Union (1714), Westminster (1717), London (1720) and Royal Exchange (1720). Other first offices were in Scotland in 1720; in the United States in Philadelphia in 1752; in Germany in 1779, France 1816 and Russia in 1827.

After the Hand-in-Hand formed

their own brigade in 1699 others followed their example. Another early brigade was formed by the Charitable Corporation who announced that they maintained 'a competent number of watermen with coats and silver badges' . . . 'carmen with carts, and porters, who give security for their fidelity, and are always to attend at fires to help remove insured goods to any place desired'. The early firemen were drawn from the Thames watermen, a practice which was to continue for the next two hundred years or so, for many of the later town brigades liked men with a maritime background; perhaps because of their great aptitude for keeping everything clean, polished and shipshape!

The second pledge of the early brigades was to protect the property and goods of the insured;

another facility which is perpetuated to this day by the Salvage Corps, who are supported by the insurance companies and are swiftly on the scene after a fire to minimise damage and loss to the insured goods.

Another very early brigade (1710) was the Sun's and the fact that the Sun had their own fire brigade to protect property that they insured was categorically mentioned in the early insurance proposals:

For the farther Encouragement of all Persons there are actually employed in the Service of the Office Thirty lusty able-body'd firemen who are cloath'd in blue Liveries and having Silver badges with the Sun Mark upon their arms, and twenty able Porters likewise, who are always ready to assist in quenching fires and removing goods, having given Bonds for their Fidelity.

Yet another fire office stated that 'For the encouragement of persons insuring, proper fire engines are provided and a number of engineers and firemen employed'.

To make the private insurance brigade firemen distinctive, smart liveries or uniforms were provided and a large badge displayed to prove the wearer's fidelity. One brigade had blue coat, cap and breeches edged in red; another preferred dark brown with red and yellow striped waistcoat, while the Caledonian had jacket and trousers of blue with inlays and turnups in orange and with an orange thistle on the front of the helmet and the name Caledonian. In Kent, each man was supplied with a silver badge depicting the Kentish Horse and a glazed black seal skin hat; and in Gloucester the uniform was blue with red facings and brass buttons and a brass helmet.

Phoenix firemen were clothed in crimson cloth lined with green, while the Westminster men had a royal blue jacket with gold cuffs and braiding, black knee breeches, gold garters and white stockings! Not to be beaten, the Royal Exchange had a uniform of yellow lined with pink, but this proved unsuitable in use and was later replaced with pea green jacket and plush breeches and vests with gilt buttons.

Below, left: A Royal Exchange fireman of the early 19th century; from a contemporary painting.

Below: Sun fireman, from W. H. Payne's 'Costume of Great Britain' (1808), with a combined treadle and manual engine in the background.

Facing page, above: Fire insurance plates from the London Fire Brigade Museum.

Facing page, below left: London Assurance fireman, 18th century.

Facing page, below right: Westminster fireman; from an 18th-century painting.

Sun Fireman. From W. H. Pyne's "Costume of Gt. Britain" (1808). Note the combined treadle and manual engine in the background.

In the early days of organised fire-fighting there were some punitive regulations attached to being a paid fireman. Fines were imposed for cursing or swearing, or for wearing the uniform when not on duty or for walking out on Sunday, for being drunk, for throwing water over another fireman or for not attending the funeral of a colleague.

In the instructions for extinguishing fires a fireman was urged to 'make the greatest haste to get on his jacket and helmet – and proceed to the engine house . . . '. The first fireman who 'gives the alarm, and orders out the horses shall have two shillings and sixpence over and above his wages'. Upon arrival at the fire:

the first object is to choose a situation for the Engine to play from, and on doing this, whenever it is possible, it is desirable to get to the windward

of the premises on fire, the current of air greatly assisting the discharge of the water in a dense column, whilst playing against the wind scatters the water and greatly diminishes its force.

A canal, tank or reservoir are to be preferred to play from when the pipes or leather hose will reach; when they will not reach, recourse must be had to the plugs of the Water Works Company. The fireman who arrives second at the Engine house should give notice of the Fire to the nearest Turncock.

The foreman should as early as possible send notice of the Fire to the Officer, and obtain Copies of Policies as to any or what property is insured with the (Society), and on receipt of the particulars must appoint a guard or such other means as appear best calculated to preserve the stock, furniture, building or other

U17179

Left: Firemen of Stuttgart in a Mercedes-Benz cross-bench-seated vehicle turn out in 1928.

Above, left: London firemen at drill, showing the smoke helmet in use around 1900.

Above, right: Firemen at drill with a horse-drawn turntable-ladder.

property, insured with the Society.

The firemen are at all times to keep in view that the Fire Engine Establishment is the property of, and is supported at the Sole expense of the Society, and therefore is not subject to the control or orders of the Police, Military, or any other person or persons whatsoever, that the orders of the foreman, and in his absence of the Fireman in command of the Fire Engine, are at all times to be explicitly obeyed.

The Foreman, or Fireman, in command of the Engine is to remember that when premises are on fire they are the property of the Office in which they are insured, and therefore he must act according to his own judgement as to the best means of preserving the property in danger.

The above instructions were from old records of the Norwich Union Fire Office and similar regulations of the London Assurance urges their firemen to note:

That at all Alarms of Fire, where an Engine is necessary the

Firemen and Porters do take Care, that one or more of the Engines belonging to the Corporation, be forthwith conveyed to the Place where the Fire is, in order to extinguish the same.

That the Firemen and Porters at all Alarms of Fire, do make haste to the Place where the Fire is, using their best endeavours to extinguish the same and to save any Goods in Danger.

That the Firemen wear their Badges, and have their Certificates always about them to distinguish them . . . and all Firemen and Porters are to have the Number of their Badges affixed in White upon the Sleeves of the Waistcoats, that in case they work in the Waistcoats at

Fires, they may be known . . .

That no Fireman shall causelessly deface, pull down or destroy any Thing whatsoever, that is not apparently necessary for preventing the spreading of the Fire.

That the Firemen or Porters, who behave themselves courteously, and with Diligence and Fidelity, may accept Money that is voluntarily offered and given, leaving Notice thereof in Writing, with the Secretary or some of the Clerks in the Office, in Twenty-four Hours; but shall not exact, ask for, or demand any Money from any suffering Person (or that is likely to suffer); nor shall they favour any Person for Reward, Promise, or Threat, in securing his House, preferable to another's; but apply themselves for the Security of that which is most exposed to Danger.

So we can see that the early organised fire-fighters were left in no doubt as to their duties and responsibilities, but from all accounts they were a fearless bunch of men, many of whom went on to serve in the later fire brigades formed by public authorities when the insurance companies faced highly mounting costs as towns grew in size and

risks grew as life became more industrial.

The fact that the early fire-fighters came from watermen probably indicates that a man used to handling boats on a tidal river was considered right for hauling the fire engine to the fire, seeking out his water supply, pumping manually for perhaps long stretches at a time, and being of the stature and fortitude to perform rescues if required. Judging by some of the regulations mentioned earlier he probably required to act with a certain amount of authority and firmness in his dealings on behalf of his company especially when telling the police that it was his fire and he wasn't taking orders from them! All this in a smart green and yellow uniform, a silver badge on his arm and his certificate at the ready!

According to some writers of the nineteenth century it was a pity that the system of selecting volunteers for local fire companies was not as stringent as it appears to have been for the insurance brigades. In his *Fires, Fire Engines and Fire Brigades* C. F. T. Young writes a long and detailed account of the trouble experienced at the hands of volunteer firemen in America. He had much praise for the manner in which American

Above, left: Firemen display their skill at using a turntable-ladder to rescue people trapped in a high building. In this demonstration a scaffolding tower is used to simulate the building.

Above, centre: Firemen at drill with a canvas chute from the drill tower.

Above, right: Firemen damping down and checking shop premises after a serious fire at Hanwell, London, 1971.

Facing page: Two pictures capture the scene of an emergency in 1976 when a fully laden road tanker exploded in a Bedfordshire village.

society generally had taken to forming volunteer brigades, believing it to be far advanced of anywhere else in the world at that time, 1865. He was impressed by a parade that took place in Philadelphia in October of that year at which there were about 20,000 volunteers present. Each company had brought a piece of equipment – steamer, manual, hose-carriage or ladder-truck – and the parade took three hours to pass! He was full of admiration for the zeal and efficiency with which the volunteer companies operated, being most laudable about the exceptionally fine equipment which was handsomely decorated and kept in perfect condition by the volunteers.

His admiration turned to sharp criticism however when the subject of the riots which took place in Boston and Philadelphia earlier were mentioned. Evidently there was little or no selection for members of the volunteer brigades and all kinds of men were admitted, some of whom appear to have been more interested in politics than in fire-fighting.

So great did the problem become that town authorities took it upon themselves to set up proper, paid fire departments with modern equipment which needed fewer men than the old manual pumps. By introducing a modern steam pump which required but a handful of men for its operation, it was possible to dispense with two or three of the old manual pumps. By adapting the ladder-trucks to horse traction there was a saving in men needed to draw them, and in other ways the fire companies were given a new lease of life; but not without incurring the wrath of some of the displaced men who wanted revenge for being ousted from their positions.

In continental Europe there existed side by side volunteer companies and regular paid brigades. In some countries — Holland for instance — there had been full-time brigades in the larger towns while the protection of smaller towns and villages was left to volunteers. Switzerland used volunteers both in large towns and the villages but the system was taken seriously with groups of men forming themselves into well-organised companies with duties allocated and practice drills carried out.

Denmark had the town firemen drawn from the local militia while those in the smaller towns were volunteers organised on military lines. Elsewhere, as in Oldenburg, it was the responsibility of local authorities to provide firemen and equipment. Belgium had a mixed system with the brigade for Antwerp being based on the French military 'Sapeurs Pompiers' and the provincial towns relying on volunteers. Saxony had a system of police fire brigades who also carried out fire prevention work by visiting buildings and verifying that construction was not contrary to the building regulations. Hanover had a proper system of paid fire brigades, and Russia found fire-fighters from among military defaulters!

Britain had mainly a volunteer system in the nineteenth century in addition to the insurance brigades already mentioned; and towns and villages all over the country gradually joined the ranks of those seeking to obtain protection. Some towns appointed 'persons to take charge of the engine' either on a retained or full-time basis, while in other places the parish purchased a small manual engine and kept it by the church in readiness. The standard of the local fire company varied widely, often revolving around the ability of the appointed or volunteer chief to inspire his volunteers to a better level of efficiency.

In Scotland, Edinburgh formed the first municipal brigade in Britain in 1824 and James Braidwood, who became legendary in fire-fighting, was appointed its first chief. He carefully chose his men from tradesmen such as slaters, house carpenters, masons, plumbers and smiths believing that men experienced in these

trades were well used to climbing about on buildings, knew the layout and construction of buildings well and, being used to working outdoors in all weathers, could better stand the rigours of fire-fighting. No doubt Braidwood's own background of being trained as a surveyor and being the son of a builder had something to do with his choice of men, but his choice proved well founded and the brigade gradually acquired a reputation for being efficient and well trained. The latter quality was important to Braidwood and he proclaimed that his fire-fighting team could only be as good as their standard of training. Training was almost a fetish with him and he conducted a large part of it by night on the basis that most fires occurred at that time. It is reported that he also tried the use of a speaking trumpet to issue orders above the noise which usually accompanied a fire, but rejected it in favour of a bosun's whistle by which he gave coded instructions to his men. This is interesting in view of the great attachment to the speaking trumpet by fire companies in America.

More interesting is the fact that Braidwood voiced an opinion against the early steam pumps despite the good account that Braithwaite's gave of itself at a fire at the Argyll Rooms in London in 1830.

After taking up his job in London as chief of the London Fire Engine Establishment Braidwood proceeded to shape his team as he had in Edinburgh. However, he was taking over an established number of firemen who had seen service with the ten insurance brigades which went to make up the new London Establishment and he decided that seamen were to be preferred to the slaters and carpenters for, although they might need instruction and training in building construction and layout, they were well used to obeying orders, working day and night watches and generally accepting the idea of living on the job. A sign of the times was the adoption of

a plain uniform of grey coats and trousers with black leather helmets, gone were the flamboyant uniforms of the previous independent insurance offices.

Another interesting aspect of the period was that the rescue of persons from fires was given a boost by the setting up of Escape Stations in London where a wheeled escape-ladder was positioned each night in the charge of a Conductor. He was provided with a small shelter and a uniform of tarpaulin coat and trousers together with helmet, lamp and a rattle to summon help to push the escape. So we see that the rescue of persons was separate from the fighting of the fire.

With the country covered in a haphazard way some independent bodies set about forming their own brigades. Large industrial companies bought engines and had teams of employees trained in their use, and wealthy landowners took to protecting their country estates with far better equipment than many local authorities could afford.

Later in the century (1866) after the Metropolitan Fire Brigade had been formed in London and Captain Shaw had become its chief (Braidwood had been killed at the Tooley Street fire in 1861), Shaw decided to adopt the brass helmet originated by the Sapeurs Pompiers in Paris. Other brigades followed suit and the helmets became synonymous with fire uniform for very many years although not all brigades used them. In fact they proved very dangerous in use and several firemen lost their lives through the metal helmet touching live electric wires in burning buildings. They started to lose favour during the 1930s and ended up on sideboards as souvenirs. Today they are avidly collected by fire brigade enthusiasts and restorers of old equipment to such a degree that glass-fibre replicas are being made !

Today's fire-fighter is something special. Although the old-established qualities of strength and courage, skill and daring still

hold good, the highly developed technical age has brought demands for additional outstanding features in the fireman's make-up and training. His skill at fire-fighting is helped by the most modern equipment, but more important is his ability to recognise important features of any fire and know which method or equipment is best. Visits to establishments in his area, drills at factories, plants and locations together with instruction on how to approach, tackle and extinguish certain types of fires are his training.

No two places are alike and the risks vary from plant to factory, from installation to warehouse, from building site to dockyard. A fireman might be on the roof of a house at one time using plain water to douse a chimney fire, and an hour later find himself wearing breathing apparatus and using CO_2 in a smoke-logged basement. The next call could be to an overturned tanker where he must have knowledge of the liquid that is flooding into the drains and sewers, what damage it can cause, and how best it can be washed away, soaked up, dispersed or otherwise neutralised. Yet another call finds him handling a small hand-extinguisher on an electrical fire in a palatial office block full of expensive computer equipment.

His role in rescue is perhaps simpler because he has more complicated and powerful tools at his disposal, although the risks increase as life becomes more surrounded by mechanical devices. Again, the situations are innumerable. On one occasion hydraulic jacks and inflatable air-bags have to be positioned before lifting a heavy piece of equipment off a man trapped by his leg. The next call could be to a lift that is stuck with no power, requiring it to be laboriously

Right: A famous Sydney fire: the burning of Anthony Hordern's building in July 1901, from a photograph by the Australian Historical Society of Fire Engines.

wound up or down by hand so that the occupants can escape. Another day, two men are trapped by the collapse of several tons of rain-sodden earth in a trench, and the fireman must carefully decide what the chances are of getting to the men and bringing them out safely. He will have to liaise with the site engineer and look at the possibility of excavating again and shoring, digging straight down and lifting, passing air-lines, perhaps getting a doctor down to the men, and then rescue lines or a stretcher to effect safe removal. Yet another call is to a serious road accident where cutting tools have to be used to remove a damaged car from around its occupant.

So it goes on, with every fire-fighter doing his best to see that when an emergency arises he is ready and that his drills and training stand him in good stead to rescue people and keep damage to a minimum.

But fire-fighting and rescue are not the whole of the job.

Fire-fighters are called upon to lecture a workforce on fire prevention and the handling of extinguishers, or to address a class of schoolchildren on the dangers of matches, open fires, paraffin heaters, furnaces, and domestic appliances. Inspection is carried out to check that earlier recommendations have been heeded, or advice is given about means of escape from a small hotel, or multi-lingual fire alarm notices in a factory.

The life of a fire-fighter is exacting and not all the people aspiring to the job are accepted. Levels of acceptance vary from place to place although a good standard of physical fitness is a prerequisite to success. A typical recruit for the fire service would be a young man from eighteen years up to about thirty. He would be physically A1 with a high standard of eyesight and hearing. Tests of physical fitness would be given in order to test his strength over long periods, particular

attention being paid to his ability to carry another person of about the same weight over a distance in a specified time

He would be intelligent enough to have a quick understanding of verbal instructions and be able to carry them out. Written instructions must be easily understood, and the ability to write clear, concise reports is desirable. As well as practical training, drills and lectures, a lot of the groundwork for advancement is by personal study and our candidate should be able to assimilate and commit to memory many pages of

Below, left: Firemen position a wheeled escape in order to check a four-storey building.

Below: A modern Magirus turntable-ladder complete with rescue cage demonstrates its capabilities before a high block of flats.

Right: The modern fireman is called to rescue people in grave danger from a fire in a motor car.

instructions, sheets of data and reams of information on subjects as diverse as building regulations, hazardous chemicals, hydraulics, power tools, and the equipment he has to use.

Should he be up to standard on the initial physical and intelligence tests and be found to be of good character and stable background, the next move might be to a training school for a period of three to six months. Here he will be given the theoretical and practical knowledge needed by a member of the fire service. There will be classroom sessions, lectures, visits, film shows, demonstrations and much practical training, demonstrations and drill plus physical exercise. He will be shown how to recognise the various kinds of fire and rescue situations and which equipment and methods need to be used. He will be shown hand-extinguishers, small-bore hose, large hose, branches, couplings, nozzles, standpipes,

hydrants, suctions, hook-ladders, ground-ladders, aerial-ladders, wheeled escapes, turntable-ladders hydraulic platforms, water-towers, pumps, foam generators, smoke extractors, lifting equipment, cutting equipment, breathing apparatus, resuscitation equipment and plenty more. Time will be spent handling, using, climbing, testing and looking at every piece so that it becomes an everyday familiar part of his life.

Our recruit will be closely watched during his period of training, and be subjected to tests and reports on his progress. At the end of the training he will be interviewed, and in the light of his behaviour and accomplishments told whether he is finally accepted.

With the initial training over successfully our recruit then passes to an operational station as a probationer, probably for a period of about a year. Here at the station he will be one of the team, ride the apparatus and perform all the duties allocated, but he is

really still undergoing training and will be constantly watched and assisted by the senior man in the crew and by the station officer. At the end of this probation period he will again be interviewed and his record studied.

Advancement is up to the individual. If he is keen and willing he can gather all the experience possible, perhaps by moving stations to gain additional knowledge in particular areas of fire-fighting. Because theory is equally important he must study in his spare time in preparation for examinations either within his own organisation or through an outside body to gain suitable qualification.

Often progress to senior rank in large fire departments is by selection. So, if our fire-fighter wants to exchange his rubber boots and hard hat for a pair of shoes and a soft cap he must study and improve his qualifications and be seen to be a good fireman with particular qualities.

A fire engine that starts fires is an advanced method of dealing with spreading ground fires such as those occurring in forest and bush. The theory behind this startling apparatus is that if the vehicle can get ahead of the fire it can spray fire-retardent material along a line and then start a backfire towards the approaching wall of fire. By this manoeuvre there will be no combustible material left to burn in the path of the fire and it should burn itself out.

The fire-truck itself is as unusual as its fire-fighting concept. Based on an eight-wheel layout with an articulated joint in the centre the vehicle is extremely flexible and with large-section cross-country tyres is capable of crossing the wild terrain often associated with brush fires.

Produced by Lockheed Ground Vehicle Systems in collaboration with the Bureau of Land Management the truck is powered by a 210 hp Caterpillar diesel driving through a five-speed Allison automatic transmission to all four axles. Tanks hold 850 gal (3,860 l) of water and 200 gal (910 l) of fire-retardant compound, and there are ground-nozzles, a remote-control turret, two reels of 200 ft (61 m) of ¾ in. (19 mm) booster line and a flame-thrower. A separate 91 hp Detroit Diesel engine powers the 250 gal/min (930 l/min) Hale pump.

In recent years the skyline of some of our larger cities has changed because of the greater use of tower blocks, skyscrapers or high-rise buildings. Call them what you will, these buildings have brought fresh problems to people who control fire-fighting establishments and organise the forces. Fire-fighting usually takes second place to rescue and rescue is no fun in a building containing perhaps around a thousand people

Below: The best type of cross-country fire truck is one that is fully tracked.

all on little shelves stretching up and away above the maximum height of available rescue ladders and hydraulic platforms. A forty feet (twelve metre) ladder looks insignificantly useless against a forty-storey building.

So, the rescue has to be tackled from within the building, so long as access is possible to the lower floors and it is possible for those above the fire either to get up to the roof for rescue by helicopter or to be reached through the area of the fire.

Often, an ordinary thing like walking into the building is made difficult by the planners and architects, for many buildings do not front onto streets as all used to. Instead they are surrounded by pedestrian walkways, piazzas, shopping precincts and the like with perhaps vehicular access limited to a subterranean loading bay.

Inside the building other problems manifest themselves – who knows how many people are in a forty-storey hotel/office complex/suite of flats? If there are people to be rescued from the twenty-ninth floor, how many stairs will there be? Then there is the problem of being unfamiliar with the building – especially the type where one floor looks very much like all the others.

There has been a trend in modern architecture to employ great expanses of glass and plastics to enshroud the tower frame. That looks very nice in the evening sunshine, but start a fire and the heat within the building causes the glass to splinter into the street below or send hot plastic over the adjoining rooftops. The fire-fighter groping along in the dark smoke is suddenly likely to find himself walking into space.

Even trim and furnishings have gone into the plastics age, with the result that a large tower block could contain the equivalent of a warehouseful of polystyrene, polyethylene, polyvynil chloride, polyurethane besides the usual timber cotton-wool and mountain of paper.

Ship fires are another special category of fires with which the fire service has to deal and they can range from a faulty gas burner in a cabin cruiser to a giant blaze involving an oil tanker and thousands of tons of oil.

Naturally, larger ships have their own arrangements and installations for fighting fires which may be adequate when there is a full complement of crew aboard and the fire is discovered in its early stages. But a fire often starts when the ship is in dock for loading or unloading and some of the crew are on shore-leave or at least off the ship. Many fires in ships occur when they are undergoing repair or refitting, or in dry dock when there

Below: Scammell 6 x 6 high-output foam tender for the protection of an oil installation.

is a minimum of crew aboard and often the ship's services are out of action.

Some of the problems of dealing with ship fires arise because of a lack of knowledge of layout. Another is the multitude of mixed cargo that may be carried at one time. The quick spreading of heat through the steel hull can easily start additional fires, as can the movement of hot gases along gangways and through ventilation shafts. The possible upset of stability if too much water is put into certain parts of the ship has to be watched closely, and this water may have to be pumped out again or holes made in the ship's side to release it if there is danger of the ship capsizing.

There is also the risk of parts of the cargo that are not on fire being damaged by water reaching

them, and this must be guarded against. Another difficulty is being able accurately to pin-point the base of the fire on board a ship, for the heat and smoke may travel a long way along passageways and shafts before coming into the open. Sometimes there is the difficulty of being able to put water onto the fire at all, for in a large hold the fire may be well away from the hatch opening, or even well to one side so that a jet from a hose is unable to hit directly.

When a fire department has high-risk docks in its area the crews will be trained in this special sphere of fire fighting, and drills will take place in the dockland area in close collaboration with the dock owners. Where possible, ships will be visited in order to acquaint the crews with the layout of various types of ship –

Top, left: A Volvo/Skuteng 6 x 6 foam tender in action.

Top, right: A Mercedes-Benz with Total equipment for use at large chemical plants and oil installations.

Above, left: Type GMR2000/4500 Camiva body and equipment on a Berliet chassis GR280 for the protection of oil refineries.

Above, right: A heavy rescue squad on a cab-over Ford chassis, 1969.

Facing page: Camiva-equipped fully tracked vehicle ideal for fighting grass and bush fires in remote places.

passenger carrying, general cargo, bulk cargo, tankers and grain ships, etc. All have their peculiar layout and it is important to know which way the various decks, walkways, holds, ladders, companionways, shafts, tanks and so on are arranged in different kinds of ships.

Some dock and harbour authorities have their own fire departments who are specially trained in the handling of ship fires. There may be fixed installations in such high-risk areas as oil terminals, as well as fire-boats and booms, to tackle and contain blazing oil floating in the docks.

The local fire department might also carry some special items of equipment ready for any ship fire that has to be tackled. Rotating nozzles, angled nozzles, large quantities of CO_2 or steam, portable pumps, small portable boats and floating booms are all items of use in dealing with ship fires. Large quantities of foam will be required for all fires, and a fire on a ship in dry dock might require great lengths of hose to reach back to adequate water supplies.

Portable pumps might have to be used to pump water out of the ship to avoid the risk of capsizing, and clean hydrant water will be better than polluted dock water if there is the chance of damage to cargo through indiscriminate use of large quantities of water.

Forest and bush fires are often the biggest and longest-burning fires with which a fire department has to deal. Every long, dry period brings an outbreak in some heavily wooded area or vast grassland and scrub region which, if not contained within a short while, becomes a major fire with scores of apparatus being summoned together with other local emergency services, including rescue and ambulance services if life is threatened. If the blaze reaches large proportions it may be fought by the armed forces, national guard,

private brigades and volunteers, the public often lending a hand with beaters, especially if their homes are in danger. It is often the forestry authority who first gives the alarm through one of its watch-tower look-outs, and it may be the first to act with its own fire service.

With such large conflagrations weather and natural obstacles can play a great part in the spread or control of the blaze. The wind is particularly instrumental in the progress of a fire; a sudden change of direction can catch fire-fighters unawares and in a matter of moments cause them to be completely surrounded by a wall of fire. Sometimes a change in the direction of the wind can help by turning the fire back the way it came, so causing it to burn itself out because of the lack of fuel.

Shortage of water is often the most difficult aspect of fighting those fires which occur far from good roads and natural water supplies. Then the use of water-tankers or relay pumping is imperative. Hose-lines and apparatus are always vulnerable in these types of fires and there have been cases of pumps and equipment being quickly engulfed by a sudden change in the direction of the fire.

Fire-breaks both natural and man-made are often the only answer to fires covering large areas of grassland and timber. Although forestry authorities make breaks as a matter of course, a high wind can carry burning embers far over such breaks and render them useless. Often the fire department will call up earth-moving equipment to make a gigantic scar across the ground in front of the oncoming wall of flame, but it takes time to get such pieces of equipment into the fire area and the last part of the journey might be through areas not normally passable by wheeled vehicles. There are some fire services who carry in their fleet a large low-loader together with bulldozer or bucket loader ready for such emergencies, and these items of equipment may prove useful in other emergencies such as floods, collapse of earthworks or buildings, and in handling large quantities of coal or waste paper.

Often the best way of tackling fires spread over a large area is from above with aircraft, but the drawback is the amount of water that can be carried in any but the largest aircraft, and then there are the problems of low-level approach and speed of passing. Helicopters are valuable in getting men and equipment to difficult places, while large aircraft are used to drop fire-retardent mixtures well in advance of the wall of fire.

Ground vehicles used for fighting

such fires can of course be of the normal type especially where the fire is near to roads or firm tracks. For more inaccessible places something lighter with all-wheel drive and a high ground clearance is more useful. Ideally half-track or fully tracked vehicles should be used and some fire authorities

centred in high-risk areas have such vehicles in their fleets.

Trailer-pumps and demountable-pumps can be useful for stationing by the water supply while the vehicle is taken nearer to the blaze, or in cases where access to the water's edge is difficult for the larger vehicle. Water-tankers

Right: Heavy rescue truck on a Ford Louisville chassis, 1976.

are usually essential at these fires, although unless of generous capacity they are soon emptied by a modern high-output pump.

A vehicle designed for the protection of oil installations at Gothenburg in Sweden was recently delivered to the fire brigade of that city. The vehicle was built as the result of close collaboration between the Gothenburg Fire Brigade, AB Brand & Sakerhetstjanst of Stockholm and Skuteng A/S of Oslo, Norway.

Specification
Chassis: Volvo F89-38 6×4
Engine: Volvo TD120 360 hp

Transmission: Allison HT70
Water Tank: 880 gals (4,000 l)
Foam Tank: 1,320 gals (6,000 l)
Output: Small monitor 220 gal/min (1,000 l/min)
Large monitor 880 gal/min (4,000 l/min)
Performance: 0 to 50 mph (80 kph) in 45 secs

Above: A Mercedes-Benz with Total equipment used for the protection of an oil refinery at Mannheim, Germany.

Left: A Mercedes-Benz 2626 chassis forms the base of this heavy duty Anton Ruthmann crane-boom-type of rescue platform which is shown in travelling form.

Right, top: A high-output foam tender by Savel-Kronenburg on their 6 x 6 MAC06 chassis.

Right, below: A batch of SIDES VMR809 machines based on Magirus 6-wheel chassis. These vehicles carry large monitors for the rapid discharge of vast quantities of foam.

125

The vehicle is intended to be a first-attack appliance and as such cannot function for long without back up of additional water supply from the central hydrant system, another tanker/pump or a fire-boat.

Fires and accidents in underground railways have usually meant that the fire service has had to manhandle the equipment down stairways and along passageways and tunnels before they could get to grips with the fire or attempt rescue. Recently a new type of apparatus was produced by Magirus which can be used on railway, tramway and U-bahn tracks as well as normal roads.

This dual-purpose road-rail emergency apparatus is intended to attend the scene of the emergency quickly by proceeding along the rail tracks so as to get close in to the incident – usually some distance from the normal point of access for road vehicles.

Specification

Chassis : Magirus 230D16FA 4×4
Engine : Magirus Deutz 230 hp
  V8 air-cooled diesel
Length : 26 ft 7 in. (8.1 m)
Width : 8 ft 2 in. (2.5 m)
Height : 10 ft 2 in. (3.1 m)
Weight : 15¾ tons (16,000 kg)
Performance : Max speed 51 mph
  (82 kph)

In operation the vehicle is driven in line with the rails and the hydraulically operated four-wheel rail unit is lowered onto the track until the front wheels of the vehicle are lifted clear. The vehicle can then drive off, the rear wheels providing traction. The rail unit is fitted with an extra set of brakes. The vehicle is adequately equipped with rescue equipment, including a powerful winch which can be operated from either front or rear, and an electrical generator for emergency lighting and powered rescue equipment. The body is designed with the equipment lockers recessed in from the extreme edge of the vehicle and a walkway provided for access to the equipment when working in narrow tunnels. The walkway is

Facing page: Three views of a special
Magirus appliance for use on roads or
rail tracks.

Right: The Los Angeles Fire
Department finds this bulldozer
useful for forming firebreaks in grass
or bush fires.

Below: A small Mercedes-Benz
rescue truck with a boat fitted to its
roof.

reached from the back of the cab.

Where there are rivers, canals and docks in an authority's area the fire brigade is often called upon to carry out rescues from boats. Standards of equipment vary according to the severity and frequency of emergencies on water with some brigades operating many boats, such as in Venice in Italy, while others find that a small boat with outboard motor or a powered inflatable boat will suffice.

According to the amount of use to which the boat is put, it might have a vehicle specially adapted as a boat-rescue appliance or it may merely reside on a small trailer at the station. Often the problem is of launching the boat somewhere near the emergency, and for areas having low-lying ground near the water course the low trailer will usually suffice because the boat can be manhandled into the water. For areas where there are many high walls, deep docks, sheer sides or other obstructions the use of a special vehicle fitted with a crane or derrick is a necessity.

In brigades with a high mileage of water-front it is usual for one or more appliances with boats to be stationed at strategic points. The ideal vehicle will be one that has a crane for handling the boat together with plenty of equipment useful in marine rescue work. It would ideally be equipped with a generator to power emergency tools and lighting, plus such items as life-jackets, oars, ropes, ladders, hand-tools, loud-hailer, small extinguishers, resuscitation equipment and torches. The crew would have to be specially trained or picked men with experience on boats, and at swimming and diving.

Below: An ex-military DUKW is on the roster of the fire brigade at Mestre, Italy.